Mediation Mechanisms

Mediation Mechanisms

Distributive Negotiation in Litigation

Duff McKee

Ridenbaugh Press
Carlton, Oregon
2017

MEDIATION MECHANISMS

For more information, contact Ridenbaugh Press, P.O. Box 834, Carlton OR 97111.

Printed and bound in the United States of America.

First edition July 2017

10 9 8 7 6 5 4 3 2 1

Library of Congress Cataloging in Publication Data

Duff McKee

Mediation - Negotiation

Bibliography

1. Mediation. 2. Law practice.

I. McKee, Duff. II. Title.

ISBN-13 978-0-945648-40-6 (softbound)

For more information, or to order more copies of this book, contact:

Ridenbaugh Press
P.O. Box 834, Carlton OR 97111
Phone (503) 852-0010
www.ridenbaugh.com
stapilus@ridenbaugh.com

Table of Contents

Introduction

I wrote this book about the process of settling civil lawsuits for money through negotiation. It's about tactics and strategies collected by me in over fifty years of practice, including more than thirty years on the bench and in a limited private practice, working to assist in the settlement of cases throughout Idaho and the surrounding states.

Although centered on the process of settling civil lawsuits, the techniques and strategies examined here might be used by anyone involved in a high pressure, competitive negotiation to value.

The premise of this book is that settlement of a lawsuit is as much a technical process as a trial. Both consist of discrete steps from beginning to end, both are laden with tactical and strategic mechanisms and devices, both benefit from careful planning in the implementation, and both demand thorough preparation to assure success. The goal here is to examine every part of the process and organize it all into identifiable strategies and tactics available and understandable to any competent lawyer.

The heart of the process is the negotiation itself, which is explored in exacting detail in Chapters 10 through 18. But getting to the negotiation stage requires careful preparation and planning, which is examined in chapters 3 through 9. And even before that, a critical decision has to be made in whether the trial lawyer is going to handle the negotiation directly or through a mediator, which is discussed in Chapters 1 and 2.

Chapter 1 traces the recognition of negotiated settlements as a distinct process in litigation from the earliest days of the awakening through the maturation of mediation as an established method of facilitating the process. Once the importance of settlement as a means of resolving the litigation is recognized, the central decision has to be made by the trial lawyers whether to handle the tasks directly with their counterparts or work the processes through mediation. There are substantial advantages to mediation, and Chapter 2 presents the case for that decision.

In the middle part of the book, all preliminary matters that need to be worked out in order to get a case in litigation ready for a settlement effort are covered. Chapter 3 addresses the decisions that a lawyer has to make about his or her approach to task and the mental attitude that is necessary to achieve a successful negotiation. Chapter 4 takes on fundamental consideration of the case and the economics involved. It also addresses the issue of compromise and matters of principle. Chapter 5 examines all the administrative matters necessary to a settlement effort, and the planning that is required. Chapters 6 and 7 face the steps necessary to prepare the client for the effort, and discusses what can happen if the client is not prepared.

Finally in the preliminary matters to a settlement effort, Chapters 8 and 9 are the steps necessary to analyze the case itself, starting with the critical decision on whether to take the case in the first place, and continuing into determination and assessment of damage, evaluation of risk, and timing.

The second part of the book begins with Chapter 10, which deconstructs the process of negotiation, separating each of its functions and parts from inception through resolution of all issues. The fundamental processes of a negotiation are the same whether it is conducted by counsel as a direct negotiation or through the use of a mediator in a mediation session, with the only differences being in the application. The book will explain these differences and show how each can be used to a tactical advantage. Chapter 11 is a detailed, step by step explanation of the landmarks of value that are inherent in a negotiation for settlement purposes, with Chapter 12 showing how to estimate all major elements, and Chapter 13 explaining how to identify and assess risk and its impact on settlement value. Finally on this topic, Chapter 14 presents special circumstances, and identifies special factors that may affect value.

The last part of the book, Chapters 15 through 18, defines and examines the specific techniques and methods of applying all the strategies just developed into the actual negotiation, whether in a direct negotiation or through a mediator. It explains the tactical considerations that dictate when and how to use the various applications, and explains the additional devices and tools to use to keep a negotiation alive, or to rescue it if it appears to be going awry. Included in this part is the importance of having a plan for any negotiation, how to put a plan together with some sample illustrations, and how to modify and amend the plan as the negotiation unfolds.

Lastly, as an addendum, there is the narrative of a complete mediation on a hypothetical case drawn from the author's experience, to pull everything together and demonstrate a complete, successful negotiation to conclusion through mediation.

I have been a lawyer and judge for almost 53 years. I was a deal negotiator in private practice, and carried my interest in negotiation as a means of problem solving onto the bench when I was appointed a district judge in 1985. I began conducting judicial settlement conferences in 1986, and was soon conducting conferences on cases arising throughout southern Idaho. I qualified as a civil case mediator in 1997 and retired from the active bench in 2000, continuing on as a senior judge and also entering a private practice limited to alternative dispute resolution services. In that practice, I have conducted over 1,700 mediations on general civil ligation cases, seeing, examining and applying at one time or another every one of the strategic and tactical applications of negotiation discussed in this book, all in real cases under real conditions.

These are not hypothetical methods or theoretical recommendations. These are methods and devices which, if applied carefully, in the right order and with proper preparation, will work. But like anything involved in litigation, with an aggressive opponent ready to pounce if left any opening, if any of these devices are used carelessly, without understanding or preparation, or at the wrong time, or in the wrong order, they are just as likely to result in disaster.

The takeaway here and throughout this book is the importance of knowledge and preparation. As in anything touching on litigation, counsel must know himself, know the law, and know his case thoroughly. But when entering any specific activity or process in the course of litigation, knowledge is wasted without preparation. Knowledge is power, but preparation is king.

1
Where it all came from

Changes in civil litigation

Once upon a time, say in the 1960s or thereabouts, if anyone asked an old-time litigator about his settlement strategies, the response as likely as not would be a growl that, "We don't settle our cases, we try 'em!"

There was no involvement by the judiciary in the settling of cases. Law schools were exclusively involved with preparing the prospective lawyer to try the case in court. Nothing about the process or methods of settlements was taught in law school. There were no books or journals on settlement methods or about negotiation as a means of dispute resolution. The concept of bringing in a third party to assist, such as a mediation or judicial settlement conference, was unheard of.

The overwhelming attitude of the day was that the trial was the thing, and the only cases that settled were the weak sissies that could not stand the exposure to a courtroom. All this led to some curious customs.

When I began practicing law in the mid-1960s, it was a concession of weakness to be the first one to bring up the subject of settlement. This meant that the other lawyer had to raise the subject first if the case was to get settled. This led to bizarre communications between lawyers dying to discuss settlement without either one appearing to be the first one to utter the question, "Can't we settle this?"

Attitudes began to change demonstrably in the 1970s, and by the mid-1980s settling cases was on everybody's mind. Two things were happening: (1) the cost of litigation was skyrocketing, (2) the judiciary was suddenly getting involved.

The cost of litigation

In 1938, the federal courts adopted a uniform set of civil rules that that introduced broad rights of pretrial discovery and revolutionized trial practice. Soon after the uniform federal rules came into being, the states began to amend their procedural rules to follow the federal mold. By the 1950s, most states, including Idaho, had adopted the federal model of broad rules of pretrial discovery. It took a while, but by the 1980s, trial preparation under the new rules was fully integrated as standard practice. On one hand, the lawyers were better prepared and trials were no longer the adventures they once were. Without the aspect of surprise or ambush, the outcomes of most trials were far more predictable. On the other hand, the whole works had become much, much more expensive. Sophisticated consumers of judicial services, such as liability insurance companies and large corporations, were earnestly searching for alternative methods.

Judicial intervention in settlement

By the early 1970s the Idaho judicial system had been completely reorganized from what was once a collection of justices of the peace, police courts, probate courts and county district judges into the fully integrated and unified district court system we have today. Idaho's reorganization was part of a nationwide movement to streamline the judicial system throughout the several states. An outgrowth of this was the creation of the National Center for State Courts.

This resource generated an outpouring of data that had never been available before, including precise statistics on settlements. The data provided indisputable evidence of how important settlements were to the process of civil litigation. Up to this time, the culture of the day had been for the judges to pay no attention to the matter of settlements. The obvious new thinking fostered by the data pouring forth was that the process of settlement was as important to the conclusion of the case as anything contained in the civil rules. If judges were going to take control of the civil dockets, judges should also begin to pay attention to the process of settlement. A growing number of judges began casting about for methods the judiciary could use to stimulate settlements and make the process even more predictable.

With California leading the way in the West, general litigation judges began introducing judicial settlement conferences to the process. By the 1980s, judicial settlement conferences had become mandatory in California and there was considerable pressure to make them mandatory elsewhere. The lawyers in Idaho were vigorously opposed, and the Idaho judges were at best indifferent. Some thought it might be a good idea, but most were not in favor of going against the overwhelming opposition from the lawyers. The step of following California making judicial settlement conferences mandatory in all cases by rule never went anywhere in state courts in Idaho.

However, there was a growing interest in voluntary judicial settlement conferences. I was appointed to the district bench in Idaho in the summer of 1985, was introduced to this subject at the National Judicial College that fall, and started conducting judicial settlement conferences on my cases in early 1986. When I started, there was one other judge in Idaho conducting judicial settlement conferences.

The number grew, but never to more than a handful in each district. Most judges were not interested in these conferences. This meant that the few judges that were interested took on settlement conferences for cases assigned to other judges – in addition to their regular calendars. The popularity of settlement conferences did grow, and finding time to squeeze them in became increasingly difficult. The time requirements meant longer and longer delays in order to get conferences scheduled before one of the judges who were willing. As a consequence, by the middle 1990s, lawyers began to shift to using other lawyers and retired judges for the settlement conferences rather than relying upon active sitting judges.

By the early 2000s, private mediation by attorneys and retired judges had all but taken over the market for civil case mediation. A few judicial settlement conferences were still conducted by state judges, and federal magistrates were still holding conferences in federal courts, but most of the cases seeking intervention by a neutral were handled privately.

The mediated settlement conference

When the shift to using private attorneys and retired judges rather than sitting judges to moderate settlement conferences first came along, no one knew exactly what to call the things. Calling them "judicial settlement conferences," when private attorneys were running the processes did not seem appropriate. Early on, many lawyers mixed up the term "mediation" with the term "arbitration," which is the agreed upon private process for a binding result. The magistrates handling family cases had been exploring with divorce and child custody mediation to great success, and, although the processes were completely different, the term "mediation" eventually began to take hold as applicable to civil cases in general litigation.

The confusion in terminology soon resolved itself as the term "mediation" was rapidly growing throughout the country as the preferred term for the neutral facilitation of settlements in all of civil litigation. Private mediation was catching on nationwide. The American Arbitration Association added mediation to its list of services, The Judicial Arbitration and Mediation Service, or JAMS, was started in California and soon spread to other states. Seminars and training were available in Idaho and rosters of qualified mediators were established for both state and federal courts. Opposition to judge-ordered settlement processes began to lessen, and in 1996, the civil procedure rules were amended to provide that the trial judge, on a case-by-case basis, could order the parties to seek mediation from an independent mediator on the court's list.

Private civil case mediation

By the year 2000 or thereabouts, the practice of mediation in general civil litigation had settled into a significant degree of defined and uniform shape and process. The academic world was interested and involved. Training seminars on mediation methods and practices were widely available. Books and journal articles were pouring fourth. Experts in the field abounded. There was even a movement to require certification and regulation of mediators, but no one was really interested and the idea never gathered sufficient support to get off the ground.

There were some on the national scene, principally the academic interests from various law schools, who argued for a particular definition to the term "mediation" and insisting that if the process did not meet the specifics of the definition, it could not be called a mediation. The general area of criticism was the bullying and arm twisting elements that had been the hallmark of earlier judicial settlement conferences. The purists insisted that mediation as a process had to be neutral and facilitative, and that if the mediator became directive or evaluative in any way, meaning if he or she became an advocate for a particular result or a particular order or means of progressing, the person was no longer a neutral and the process was not a mediation.

To the purist, a mediation meant a moderator who was absolutely neutral, who took no position substantively or procedurally on any issue, and whose sole function was to empower the parties to control not only the substantive decisions under examination but also the direction, pace and order of the process. The battle lines were between the transformative interests on one side and the evaluative or directive opponents on the other. This debate raged in lively fashion among the academic interests and in the organizations growing up around the practicing mediators throughout the first decade of the 21st century.

By 2010, or thereabouts, the debate largely began to subside, as trial lawyers using the mediation processes became more knowledgeable and sophisticated, and as the mediators became more skilled and versatile in their craft. In today's modern mediation, the neutral can be expected to draw upon a variety of techniques during a session, depending upon what is needed to keep things alive and moving towards an acceptable solution.

A modern mediation is frequently a multi-faceted process where the mediator is called upon to facilitate not only the major disputes at issue in the lawsuit, but also a myriad of internal disagreements which may arise en route to any solution, and from within the constituency of the various parties. The mediator may find barriers that need to be resolved in the relationship between plaintiff and his lawyer, or in the interests of and interplay between the defense counsel, his nominal client, and the insurance carrier's representative in attendance. In some instances, differences may arise between members of the client entity making up either party to the suit – husband and wife, for example, or business partners, or co-investors, who may disagree with each other or with their lawyer over some facet of the process.

There are a multitude of relationships that a mediator may face in any given case, each requiring a different approach to resolution. Moreover, a mediation may start out in a neutral manner on substantive issues but be somewhat directive on matters of process, then move into an evaluative mode to get the parties though some tight spots, and then shift back to a more transformative mode near the end, while the fine touches are worked out by the parties. The mediator needs a fine-tuned sense of when to move in and push and when to pull back and stay out of the way. It is a rare instance where a mediator will remain in the same mode throughout a mediation with respect to all the parties and as to all the issues that may be presented. Each case presents a different set of circumstances.

What is clear today is that the settlement process is now primary in the minds of most litigators and most judges. Trial calendars with multiple settings are a fact of life, with cases stacked four to six deep, with the full expectation that five out of six cases set will settle before trial.

While trial preparation is a necessity, in many cases the object of the trial preparation is to get the case in position to settle. Deferring the discussion of settlement is no longer with the expectancy of going to trial, but rather to complete the steps necessary to maximize the results at mediation. While the concept of guided settlement processes for the civil case still has a long way to go, the civil case mediation has come of age in our system. It is becoming increasingly important that this process be thoroughly understood by the participating lawyers.

2
The argument for mediation

An important decision the trial lawyer will have to make in addressing the objective of settlement is whether to take on the task of direct negotiation with opposing counsel or seek the assistance of a mediator. Because this decision can permeate almost every step in the process, this question is presented and examined here first.

Mediation is guided negotiation. The steps in the process, the methods employed, the settlement dialogue, and all of the strategic and tactical considerations are almost exactly the same whether in direct negotiation or in mediation. But although the processes appear similar, having the process under the control of a skilled neutral can make a tremendous difference.

It is an extraordinarily difficult task for most trial lawyers to shift gears mentally from being a courtroom advocate to becoming a deal negotiator. The confrontational, adversarial mental state necessary to take a case into a courtroom is completely inapposite to the cooperative, collaborative mental state necessary for a deal negotiator.

The problems inherent here leap out when the trial lawyer attempts the simple process of transmitting a suggestion to negotiate to his counterpart on the other side.

Confusing the message

Once a negotiation is started, the true strength of the negotiating dialogue is going to be in the raw numbers contained in the amounts offered and demanded for, as everybody knows, "money talks." The problem is that the lawyers talk, too, when delivering their offers and demands, and too often, the language of the lawyers gets in the way of the message contained in the raw numbers.

Let's listen to a plaintiff's lawyer try to negotiate a case directly with a tough defense lawyer. The lawsuit is a complicated, multi-count products liability claim including defect in manufacturing, defect in design and failure to warn. The exact details are unnecessary here; pay attention to style and technique.

"We'll drop our demand from $150,000 to $125,000," the plaintiff's lawyer says, "but you need to know that we are not dropping our claim that your product is poorly engineered, and we can prove it."

"The claim just isn't worth $125,000," the defense lawyer fumed. "We acknowledged the manufacturing defect in the offers we have already made, but the engineering claim just isn't there. In fact, it isn't worth the $50,000 we offered last time. If you're going to stick on that ridiculous demand with the engineering claim, we are dropping our offer to $45,000."

"What? You can't go backwards on me. What we'll do is amend to make that claim one for punitive damages."

"Oh yeah? Well, if that's where your head is, just go ahead and file the motion. We know how to read Rule 11 and we think the judge does too. If all you're going do is to waste everyone's time at this, we are out of here."

"Well, fine!"

"Fine!"

(Sound of doors banging,)

Uh oh.

We don't know where the defense might have gone here, but plaintiff's counsel made any move by the defense very difficult by coming on too strong, arguing his claim rather than focusing on the solution, labeling his moves in litigation terms and injecting a threat of punitive measures into what should have been a collaborative dialogue. By attaching labels to the numbers, the advocacy smothered the actual message and made it difficult if not impossible for defendant to make progress. Instead, the defense responded in kind, and the negotiation collapsed.

The money offer was a drop by $25,000, which should have been sufficient to send a clear signal that the offering party was interested in settling the case at some number under $125,000. It was not a drop-dead number, and it appeared to be a decent move off plaintiff's last offer. The problem was, plaintiff's lawyer did not have his head in the game. Instead of verbalizing the settlement message, or staying out of the way of the money message and saying nothing, plaintiff's lawyer weighed in with a positional attack – to demonstrate to defense counsel that he was right and the other lawyer was wrong. He didn't want to settle the case, he wanted to win it – and it derailed the process.

Introducing mediation

Mediation is the introduction of a disinterested third party to act as a go-between in the conduct of a settlement negotiation.

An essential function of mediation is that it allows both sides to maintain their individual battle positions intact while exploring the possibilities of settlement through the independent channel of the mediator. The mediator becomes a sounding board and the voice of reason as he or she moves back and forth between the parties, who are allowed to give the impression that they are both remaining in their fortified trial positions with no concessions or deviations expected unless and until the entire case is resolved, while they are in fact exploring the pieces and parts of the case to determine the collaborative possibilities of settlement.

The mediator is there to assist the parties with the process of negotiation – to be a coach or guide in constructing negotiation moves, in creating any messages that are intended or need to be included, to deliver the messages and make sure they are not misunderstood, and to facilitate the exchanges between the parties and keep it on track towards a solution.

Suppose a mediator had been involved in that confrontation presented above, over the product liability case and whether the engineering claim had merit. The personal arguments of the advocates got in the way of the message, and the negotiation collapsed. With a mediator, perhaps, the conversations might have gone like this:

Plaintiff's lawyer to the mediator in private caucus: "OK, we will drop our demand to $125,000, but you tell them that we are not dropping the engineering claim. We think this is a strong component of the case, we are convinced we can prove it, and if we go forward with this we are going to consider amending to add punitive damages."

Mediator: "OK but do you mind if I not say anything about the punitive damage claim just yet? I assume you haven't filed anything?"

Plaintiff's lawyer: "On, no. We are just thinking about that, depending on how this mediation goes. There are no punitive damages in the numbers we are sending down. And you don't have to tell them anything unless you think it would help. I just wanted you to know our position."

Mediator: "OK, let's see what happens."

Mediator goes down the hall to the defense room. "They dropped their demand to $125,000 to settle both the defective manufacture and the improper engineering claims. What do you think?"

Defense counsel: "How can they possibly think the claim is worth that much?"

Mediator: "Well, they have the manufacturing defect and they do have that claim that the device was improperly engineered. How strong do you think that claim is going to be?"

Defense counsel: "Not strong at all. Our engineering on this was right in the middle of the industry standard. It's too bad the device failed, and we understand the problem with manufacturing. We have fixed that and it won't happen again. But the defect was in manufacturing, and it is not on the engineer."

Mediator: "Do I understand you to say that you are probably going to lose on the manufacturing claim?"

Defense counsel: "Well, we haven't admitted liability yet, but it did happen the way they say. But if it's just the manufacturing claim, it's not worth anywhere near $125,000 – it's more like the $50,000 which we have already offered last time, or maybe up to $75,000. But if they are at $125,000, we are not going to budge from the $50,000 until they come down. We are too high already. In fact, I think we ought to send back $45,000.

Mediator: "And you think you will probably win on the engineering claim – but you haven't got summary judgment. Right?"

Defense counsel: "Yes, the judge said there are issues of fact, and it's going to turn on the expert testimony."

Mediator: "So the best you can say is that you will probably win the engineering claim, but it is going to go to the jury? What are your odds?"

Defense counsel: "They are great here – better 90/10 in my opinion."

Mediator: "Oh, come on. It's a jury trial. And you just told me you are probably going to lose on the manufacturing defect. After they find you at fault there, you think an average jury is going to have no problem in the pivot to giving you a get-out-of-jail-card on the other?"

Defense counsel: "Well, OK, maybe 80/20."

Mediator: "Did the judge say it was going to turn on expert testimony? How about, maybe 60/40? It is a jury issue, isn't it?"

Defense counsel: "I don't want to argue this point with you, it's a strong part of our defense, and we are just not going to put much money on it here."

Mediator: "I am not arguing the point with you either, counselor, I just want to make sure you are looking at this with your eyes wide open. How much will it cost you to try this case if you have to defend the engineering claim? In trial costs, your fees, expert fees and so forth – from this day through the end of trial?"

Defense counsel (thinking): "Um, maybe another $60,000 to $70,000.

Mediator: "So, are you telling me that you are willing to recommend that company pay an additional $70,000 in litigation costs to find out whether it can hold the loss to $75,000 on a case that might explode well above that number, even though the long odds are in your favor, and that the whole thing can be settled right now for $125,000, and probably less. Tell me how that makes any sense."

Defense Counsel: "Let me have a minute with my client."

There is no way the plaintiff's counsel could have this sort of conversation with the defense counsel if they were negotiating the case directly between them without the defense counsel telling him these questions were none of his damn business and to go jump in the lake.

A mediator can take the same message and reframe it completely in the process of carrying it from the plaintiff to the defense, and then present it in a fashion that fits with the analysis the defense really needs to concentrate on in making the decisions from their side of the table.

The process also works because the litigators do not have to mentally shift gears out of their adversarial frame of mind necessary to the litigation effort. They do not have to collaborate with each other; they only have to work cooperatively with the mediator. Cooperation with a mediator is significantly different than collaboration with the enemy. The parties do not have to be milquetoasts or doormats with the mediator, they just need to be attentive and honest. A mediator who knows what he is doing will become exceedingly adroit at extracting just what he needs to communicate the collaboration necessary to effect a settlement without requiring either party to concede anything until there is a solution at hand.

Mechanisms of a mediation

A mediator brings to the settlement venue a bag full of tools to accomplish this end. The devices are effective and can add value to the process whether both sides appear to be all geared up to do battle in court or are fully prepared and motivated to settle. All of the devices are not necessary in every case, and mediators tailor their approach by what is necessary to the actual case. Here is a catalog of the advantages to seeking intervention through mediation, even in an apparently simple case with both sides motivated and ready to settle.

The mediation venue allows the parties and counsel to explore settlement without having to abandon their positions of advocacy. By filtering the communications through a mediator, who will reframe the messages into collaborative signals more conducive to settlement, both parties can examine the settlement prospects from their battle positions as though it was the result of direct collaboration. But by using the mediator to carry the messages, and utilizing the mediator's experience as a sounding board to factor in the compromises that may be necessary, neither party risks any sort of tactical ambush that a unilateral attempt at conciliation might bring. Also, neither side risks losing a round, or the whole negotiation, because they let their mouths get in the way of the message.

Further, if the mediation does not work, the parties have not abandoned the adversarial mode necessary to the litigation process, and thus suffer no strategic or tactical loss in exploring settlement. A combination of civil rules, evidence rules, and the typical mediation agreements offer this protection by insulating the mediation process completely from the continuation of litigation.

Mediation provides an opportunity to focus on the critical issues or sticking points of the case, creating a mechanism for an objective assessment of the case from all sides of the table. When in the adversarial mode, we tend to concentrate only on the strong points of our case, and down play or gloss over our weak spots and the strengths of the other side's case. When in an adversarial mode and hearing the opposition arguments, it is human nature to listen selectively and hear only what we want to hear as we wait for the opportunity to interrupt and present our side of the argument. Too often, any examination of the other side's position is only for the purpose of preparing a rebuttal, with no one really listening. The mediator brings a fresh set of neutral eyes and ears that can guide parties and counsel to more efficient listening, reframing arguments, and eliminating or winnowing out irrelevant elements of the case, all to facilitate a more objective assessment from each side. The analysis is done in the safety of the private caucus with the mediator, with no danger of leaking anything to the opposition.

Mediation by an experienced trial lawyer or retired judge enables counsel to use the mediator's experience to test theories and arguments. While the mediator is not likely to quantify any issues, or give any specific opinion on how such will affect the outcome, the mediator will recognize the existence of valid legal issues and foresee the general framework of the potential problems. This enables counsel for each side, working independently of one another and privately with the mediator, to objectively assess the actual impact the elements and potential theories may have upon the value of the case.

Mediation offers the opportunity to work out internal differences between lawyer and client or among the clients, or between the clients and others who may be interested in the outcome – banks, investors, subrogated claimants, employees, etc. This list is not exclusive. It is not uncommon to find the lawyers considerably ahead of their clients in the appreciation of risk, or in a realistic evaluation of the case in light of emerging developments.

This can pose a difficult dilemma for a lawyer with a strong willed client. In such cases, the lawyer can use the mediator's skills and devices to assist in raising the client's level of awareness about risk and value without appearing to be taking sides against the client's wishes. As the mediation moves through the winnowing of issues, reality checking, and exercises in objective evaluation and reframing, the lawyer can work with the mediator to ensure that the mediator helps increase the client's awareness of risk and the impact on case value. The lawyer can thereby allow his client and himself to be positioned in a far more realistic collaborative stance with the mediator, without having to appear to act at cross-purposes with the client.

Advantages of Mediation

Litigation negotiation through a mediator usually is accomplished by the mediator working back and forth between private caucuses, delivering offers and counter-offers privately to the parties as they progress towards a settlement figure. Working this process of offer and counter-offer through a mediator, instead of direct communications between counsel, has many advantages:

- The mediator can assist in structuring offers and counteroffers, advising the parties and counsel in devising strategies to develop and convey intended messages about the value of the case, and about its perceived strengths and weaknesses.
- The mediator can make sure that the messages embedded in the offers and countermoves are the messages that the offering party intends to send, and in delivering the moves to the other side, can ensure that the messages are clearly understood by the receiving parties.
- The mediator can help in keeping parties focused on the objectives, and in making sure that the progress is approximately equal as the mediation progresses. It is the mediator's task to keep the pace of the mediation appropriate, and not to allow one to get too far ahead, nor to get bogged down or lost in the weeds. There are a number of mediation devices to boost a stalled dialogue, to reframe one that is going astray, or to slow down the party who has it all figured out and wants immediately to "cut to the chase."
- In practice, civil case negotiation to value works best when both sides arrive at the ultimate value at about the same time. When one side arrives at the goal too early, they may become impatient or indignant when the other side does not immediately respond in kind. This alone may cause a negotiation to break down. A mediator can prevent this mechanical breakdown by pacing the offers and counter-offers to keep both sides on track.
- The mediator can be invaluable in assisting the parties to close the deal when the objectives are at hand. There is a

great tendency in complex cases, and sometimes in not-so-complex cases, for disputants not to recognize when or how to quit negotiating – to recognize that the goal is at hand, and the time has come to close the deal and celebrate. It sometimes happens that the arrival of one party at the goal is seen by the opposition as an invitation to reset the goal and drive on. A mediator can help immensely in avoiding these traps.

- A mediator can help devise strategies to circumvent or avoid deadlock and impasse, where such is possible, or will identify the futility of further effort where avoiding deadlock is not possible. Calling a halt to the negotiation that is not working, especially when accompanied by an analysis of what went wrong, can be extremely valuable in getting the settlement effort restarted at a later time, when this is possible.
- Finally, a mediator usually has a bag of tricks to use as a last ditch effort to prevent a potentially deadlocked mediation from failing. Such last ditch efforts are usually not amenable to unilateral use, if the parties are trying to negotiate directly, without the offering party appearing vulnerable and desperate in the attempt.

Negotiation to settlement of cases in litigation is unlike any other negotiation in the market place. When haggling for a new car, for instance, the dealer and customer will usually tolerate only two, maybe three, rounds of offer and counter-offer before the deal is either on the way to the closers or called off entirely. There are too many options in the market place, and if a deal is to be struck everyone knows that the bargain has to be identified quickly.

In litigation, there are no options. The case is on the rails headed for a jury courtroom, and if the parties do not settle their case, the jury will. Calling the deal off is not an option, and attempting to postpone a decision may have immense consequences on the cost of the litigation, if it is possible at all. As a result, negotiation in litigation is highly structured. Many moves, especially at the outset, are totally tactical and say nothing about the party's true estimation or appreciation of the ultimate value. The chances of misunderstanding the intended strategy by misreading early moves are great. The transition from tactical moves to value based offers intended to be operative can be illusive and difficult to recognize. Even when the probable value is identified and apparently agreed to, movement can still be agonizingly slow as one side or the other moves in tentative steps towards closure. The use of a mediator to coach, instruct, advise and guide in the entire negotiation process can significantly avoid or alleviate all of these traps and difficulties.

Mediation's forte is the mixed risk case where there is not only the issue of damages in dispute, but also substantive issues on liability and comparative fault, and perhaps counterclaim and cross-claim issues to gum up the works. While any case can benefit from mediation, clearly the more complex cases are significantly benefited from using the third party channel to organize and manage the settlement communications.

On selecting the mediator

When counsel decides to use a mediator, this step will require either the concurrence of the opposition or a court order. In the early days, there was considerable reluctance to enter mediation on the part of a sizable number of lawyers. The custom of the time was to obtain an order for mediation upon contested motion, even though the eventual order might be by stipulation. The tenor of the trial bar has changed dramatically in recent years, and it is now seldom the case where either lawyer resists reference of a case to mediation. The only issue is not whether, but rather when and who to select.

There are lots of mediators out there, some with tons of experience and some just getting started. Also, there are a number of theories of mediation, each with its earnest cadre of academic adherents ready to advocate for their methods – transformative, facilitative, evaluative and directive to identify in very broad terms the main divisions of thought.

- *Transformative* mediation is where the mediator empowers the participants to make all necessary decisions, both as to the process of settlement and the substantive issues to be settled;

- *Facilitative* mediation is where the mediator leaves the evaluation and quantification of substantive issues to the participants, but controls the process of the negotiation;
- *Evaluative* mediation is where the mediator is involved with the evaluation of substantive issues and works to direct the negotiation towards an acceptable zone or area of settlement.
- *Directive* mediation is where the mediator knows the right answer and works to get everyone to agree with him.

At one time, while the academic debates over the various theories raged, it might have made a difference what theory the chosen mediator practiced. But in modern litigation, these differences have essentially evaporated. In a significant settlement effort, a skilled mediator will use all of these techniques during one phase or another, and as he or she works through the several layers of issues involved.

It is not uncommon to find the case presenting multiple issues for resolution, each requiring a different approach. The case itself, of course, is primary, and as it moves through the various phases of the negotiation, it may appear to track facilitative processes in general, but may take a evaluative turn or two to get it started or keep it in line, and then turn completely transformative at the very end. Along the way, issues between counsel and client may arise in the middle of the case that are best handled with an evaluative touch. If there are any onlookers present who want to get involved, this usually requires directive intervention from the mediator to keep things in line. Today's mediator is seldom an exclusive adherent of any one of the various methods or theories, but rather is facile in applying all of them when and as needed.

The selection of the mediator, then, becomes one of personal preference. Who can the parties work with the best, and who do the lawyers feel can get the job done? Usually, the lawyers select the mediator, and if they cannot agree, they can apply to the court to pick. There are court rules in all jurisdictions today covering the selection of a mediator upon application to the court, if necessary.

There is one area where a general rule might be important. In mediation of general civil litigation, if the skill level and experience of the lawyers is unbalanced, the mediator should be at least as skilled and experienced as the highest skilled lawyer involved in the process. If one of the participating lawyers outranks, or thinks he outranks, the mediator, there is the risk that there will be a turf battle over control of the process.

This is not an awful, terrible, horrible, very bad thing. It is a normal expectancy whenever strong willed litigation lawyers are involved. The ego of most skilled litigators easily approaches that of a field marshal or neurosurgeon, and if unchecked, any trial lawyer worthy of the name will instinctively move in to take over whatever endeavor they are involved in. There is some safety if the opposing lawyers are evenly matched, for even if they outrank the mediator, they will usually keep each other in check and allow the mediator to work without interference. But if there is an imbalance in skill levels among counsel – whether real or imagined – and one lawyer thinks he outranks everybody else, a control problem may develop.

This is subtle, and often a mediation will work just fine no matter who is in control, but control of the process does belong with the mediator, and if there are problems along the way, this may become important. The good mediator will stay out of the lawyers' way on matters of content and substance, but he will insist upon maintaining control of the process.

The key here is relatively simple. As a first criteria, the lawyer should select a mediator he or she likes and who can get along with everybody. As a second criteria, and whenever possible, the mediator should have a level of skill and experience that is equivalent to the highest skilled lawyer in the mix. If this cannot be done, and the mediator's skill level is less than desired, be aware of the potential for control issues.

3
Getting the lawyer's head in the game

To be very clear about this, we are talking about money and money only.

Most civil litigation is not about patching up relationships or improving morale, or reopening market opportunities. Occasionally, one will see litigation where the parties expect to continue on after the suit is resolved in some sort of relationship, but more common is the situation where the parties never expect to have anything to do with one another after the suit ends. Some litigation settlement agreements even include clauses in to the effect that the parties are never to darken each other's doors again. The overwhelming number of lawsuits involve money and money only.

If the litigation does involve any of these complex subjects, or if the elements of any solution do require consideration of relationships, or morale, or quantification of non-monetary issues, the subject requires specialized negotiation skills far beyond that expected of the trial lawyer. Family court mediators, for example, received special training that is completely different than the civil case mediation field. Negotiations and mediations in this area are for the specialists; mediation is probably essential, and counsel may well be selected for their skills at negotiation rather than trial advocacy. These issues have nothing to do with what this book is about.

This book is about litigation over matters in contract or tort – broken promise or personal injury – where the dispute is devoted to picking over the details of some event in the past that has gone wrong, either in contract or tort, determining who is to blame for screwing it up, and arriving at some figure of monetary damages to set it right and even the score. One edge of any deal to be made is going to be hard cash, and there will be little or no opportunity for creative solutions. The questions presented are straightforward evaluations of liability and damage in single, one-off events, without concern for preserving relationships, on-going or future connections between the parties, future promises of action or participation, or any other kind of consideration of continued performance, and no way to expand the box or enlarge the pie to bring in considerations other than money.

Distributive negotiation

The negotiation for money in money-damage-only cases is referred to as *distributive negotiation* – the process of identifying what amount of money, if any, is to be "distributed" from one side to the other. Distributive negotiation is considered "win-lose" or "zero-sum" negotiation, in the sense that every dollar added to one side is subtracted from the other.

The negotiation techniques of *distributive negotiation* will differ from the techniques employed in *integrative negotiation*, where the issues are broader and the possible solutions more open to creative innovation – these are the exchanges by both sides without the hard, precise edge of a money-based price being assigned to the objectives of either side. These are the supposed win-win or interest based deals, where both sides might continue to add and revise their end of the deal until a total package is arrived at that satisfies both sides. The deal might be encapsulated by the phrase, "We'll give you X if you do Y," where neither X nor Y has an established hard money price, and money is not otherwise involved.

Given this growing legal climate with its preference towards settled cases rather than trials, once we figure out that negotiation is preferable to litigation, why involve these matters in litigation at all? Why not just turn the lawyers loose with instructions to negotiate and get out of the way? Negotiation is made up of simple communications skills, which we learn intuitively as we grow up, right? If the case never starts out in litigation, then the lawyers never have the opportunity to get their heads in the wrong game. They would always be geared for settlement. Wouldn't this work better?

Two things. The main and overwhelming problem with the suggestion is that litigation is an essential "or else" to the resolution of the usual dispute that is the mainstay of civil litigation; it is an essential incentive to negotiate to a solution. Without litigation as the alternative, some disputes would never resolve – parties, counsel, hangers on, etc. would just dicker on forever. With litigation looming, however, the threat is always present. If the parties don't settle the case, the courts will. This is a necessary hammer to have over the head of most litigants to get their attention and bring them to the table.

From Adversarial Negotiation to Value

The second reason is that most lawyers are uncomfortable in negotiating to value in a high profile or pressure-cooker situation. Skills in this adversarial, competitive type of negotiation do not come intuitively, we do not learn them from an early age, and most of us do not do them well.

The negotiation skills we learn from childhood are to share, to work things out, that peaceful solutions are preferable, etc., which are all hallmarks of *integrative negotiation*. Most of us understand the concept of interest based negotiation – we practice it all the time. It is the basis for discussions with our life partners on such topics as where to go on vacation down to what to have for dinner or what program to watch on television. It requires being aware of the other side's interests and motives, of seeking answers that serve both sides equally well, or of making arrangements to balance the books if a current deal appears to be one sided, etc. We can "look outside the box," or see if there are not ways to "enlarge the pie" – meaning to redefine the subject matter of the deal to seek fairness. The objective of integrative negotiation is always a win-win outcome for both sides.

Most litigation negotiation does not fit this mold. Resolving money-damage lawsuits through negotiation involves the much harder edge of money. This means that most litigation negotiation is going to be *distributive negotiation.* And the plain fact is that most of us are not good at all in distributive negotiating to value when the pressure is on in any kind of adversarial, confrontational situation, which is the essence of litigation.

Other cultures embrace negotiation to value as part of their everyday living. Merchants in many Middle Eastern and Asian countries may be insulted if customers decline the social interaction of a friendly haggle over even routine daily purchases. We, on the other hand, are a K-Mart Society by and large. We allow someone else to establish the value – or price – of virtually everything in our lives, and then we either accept or decline depending upon our immediate needs and our internal personal value judgment. We adjust the values we pay by shopping around to different stores, or delaying our decisions until the prices change or deals are offered. What we do not do is approach the store clerk with an invitation to haggle.

"You have this bottle of ketchup marked $1.89," we would never say, "I'll give you a buck and a half to take it off your hands today – how about it?" The clerk would probably call security. In the few instances where it is customary to negotiate to value – when buying a horse or a used car, for example – most of us view the task with about the same enthusiasm as a root canal.

The reasons are cultural and environmental. In pressure situations, where the heat is on, where the objective is important or the values are significant, we are not comfortable in negotiating to value. If there is not a price tag or declared value to weigh and accept, we are more comfortable in allowing someone else to decide the value, and set the eventual price, and leave us to either accept or reject. Some of us will look for a new job rather than attempt to negotiate a higher salary at the job we have; we move rather than taking the landlord on when he threatens to increase the rent.

One reason for this is that we did not grow up with collaboratively competitive negotiation in confrontational situations; instead, we learned the methods of what we now recognize as adversarial advocacy. Recall the times when we were four or five years old, and found ourselves in some sort of squabble with a playmate or sibling. Recall that if the squabble was trivial, Mom would insist that we work it out among ourselves, but if the values were important and the pressure was on, Mom would drag the dispute into the kitchen, try the case, and lay down the rule.

We learned at a very early age that when the values were important and the heat was on, the essential manner of resolution involved transferring responsibility for the decision to Mom and then persuading her that we were right, or innocent, or deserved more. This mode of high-pressure adversarial communication carried itself into the classroom to disputes refereed by the teacher or vice-principal, and later into the workplace and to disputes adjudicated by the boss or supervisors. And, of course, this is the very essence of our judicial system. As lawyers, we continued to hone and refine the mechanisms for dispute resolution in the courtroom, ignoring completely the concepts of objective assessment, competitive collaboration, and conciliation - the necessary tools of the deal negotiator.

The communication model just described is the classic advocates' triangle, with advocates at the base corners aggressively advancing their best case to the decider – be it judge, jury, arbitration panel or other decision making tribunal at the apex.

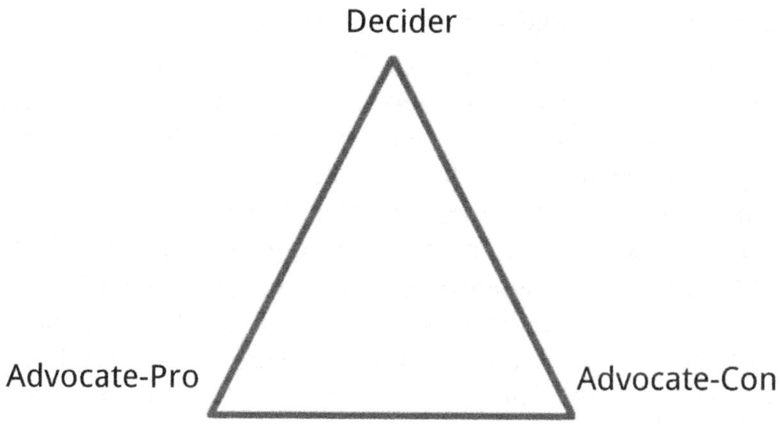

This method of communication works great in any adjudicative forum where there are strong advocates at each corner of the base to advance the alternative and opposing arguments of the case, and where there is an entity at the apex of the triangle to hear the arguments and make a ruling – whether it is Mom, the vice principal, a supervisor in the workplace, an arbitrator, a commission or board, or a judge and jury. This communication tool is the quintessential skill of the trial lawyer in the litigation arena where victory or capitulation are the expected objectives.

The skills break down, however, when the objective is collaborative communication across a settlement table without a Mom at the head to keep things in order. Where the objective is collaboration, the assertive, aggressive and confrontational mode of communication appropriate to the adversarial advocacy process is not only ineffective but is usually counterproductive.

The conflict between skills

For effective settlement negotiations, it is essential for the lawyer who is to become the negotiator to shift gears out of the adversarial mode and move toward a collaborative mode of communication with the opposing counsel. This is easy to say, but difficult and counter-intuitive for both lawyers and clients to accomplish in the midst of actual litigation.

In an exercise at a seminar on negotiation, the presenter got everyone on their feet and counted off into pairs. Then he gave the following instructions: "Draw an imaginary line between you and your opposite, and, in the time allowed, convince your partner to step over the imaginary line. You may not touch or threaten or use force of any kind. Just talk. Two minutes." The trial lawyers were singularly unsuccessful. They viewed the objective as winning the exchange, which meant getting the adversary over to their side of the line. Most failed completely. A few succeeded by bribing the other party with something tangible – a drink after, or a favor of some kind – and a few even offered cash. But in the majority of pairs, both talkers remained on their own side of the line when the presenter called a halt. The negotiators had no problem with the exercise. They looked at the problem objectively, and examined carefully the result expected – which said nothing of there being a winner or that they had to stay on their own side of the line. So they simply switched position with their partners, with both partners being easily talked into "stepping across the line." Notice nothing in the instructions said anything at all about the need for the parties to wind up on the same side of the line – nothing, in other words, prevented each from giving the other exactly what was asked.

The difference was in their inherent approach to the issue of dispute resolution. The litigation approach to dispute resolution is to marshal the facts, organize the case to emphasize the strongest points, ignore or bury the unfavorable parts, and press the case to a third party decider – jury, judge, arbitrator or whoever – with the objective of "winning" a decision from the decider. Settlements are approached the same way. The objective is a capitulation, with the other side having to concede defeat and agree to meet the demands being presented. To the trial lawyer, both the trial and the settlement process are zero-sum games, with every concession given up being a mini-defeat. To the trial lawyer, the move by the opponent to "step across the line" was a concession of defeat, and one that certainly could not be reciprocated. The negotiator sees no such obstacle to the process; he is not burdened with the necessity of "winning" the exchange and does not see any move on his part as a "concession." The negotiator thinks only, "What can I give my partner that she needs in order for her to give me what I need to make this work?" Once the answer becomes obvious, the problem is over.

The issue of the lawyer as negotiator is further complicated because each of the participants involved in litigation, even those on the same side of the table, usually have a different stake in the outcome. Certainly the lawyers for each side must keep the best interests of their clients foremost, but notwithstanding their ethical and professional duties to their clients, the lawyers invariably have their own direct and personal stake in the dispute, if nothing more than from the standpoint of their professional reputations. Where client and counsel agree on the case and all facets of it, any differences between them may be insignificant. But where lawyer and client do not see eye to eye on all aspects of the case, whether in the probable outcome or even in some relatively minor aspect of it, these differences may influence the settlement process. Further, where the lawyer has a direct economic interest in the case, such as contingent fee, or significant costs that have been advanced or are to be advanced if litigation is to continue, internal issues between lawyer and client can confound the most dedicated professional.

The litigator approaches the process of dispute resolution with the objective of winning. The negotiator's objective is not losing. The theoretically ideal negotiated settlement is where both sides are satisfied that they have "not lost" their side of the case by exactly the same measure.

The negotiator marshals the facts and evaluates all the strong points of one side, just as in litigation. But the negotiator does not ignore or bury the unfavorable parts. These must be marshaled and evaluated right along with the strong points. There is no third party to decide the thing, so an agreement must be reached with the other side. Unless the case is a true slam-dunk, expecting outright capitulation is too much – the negotiator has to find avenues for mutual agreement – in a word, compromise. This means the negotiator cannot just press the strong parts of the case, he must accept and balance other parts of the case as well.

Of equal importance, the negotiator must listen and take into account what the opponent wants and needs in the outcome of the case, and harmonize the differences if at all possible. If it is not possible to objectively harmonize the differences, then the negotiator must assess the risks of each position as it may affect the eventual outcome, and incorporate the risks into the objective evaluation of the case. To start looking for compromise.

When trial lawyers negotiate through correspondence, they seldom curb their zeal for advocacy in the letters they write. The demand letter to defense counsel will be loaded with arguments on how strong the plaintiff's case will be, how weak the perceived defenses will prove to be, and the inevitability of a huge jury verdict. The defense reply will be equally strident in pointing out the legal mistakes and erroneous assumptions, and the certainty of a much reduced verdict, and perhaps even a clean defense victory. Lost in the grandiose verbiage might also be the elements of some offers and replies.

In reality, the exposition of advocacy in outlining the dire consequences that will befall the opposition if immediate capitulation to the demand is not forthcoming is a waste of time, and is singularly unproductive. Opposing counsel does not need to be lectured on the law, or upon the impact the case may have upon a jury, or upon the certainty of any judgment for the huge amounts demanded. Throwing adjectives around here is equivalent to following the collaborative offer with a Molotov cocktail; all that is engendered is an equally inflammatory and venomous reply.

In correspondence, all that is needed in the initial demand is a spare, adjective-free recitation of the core facts to make sure both sides have the same basic elements in mind, and the number. Leave the argument out. Leave the bombastic conclusions out. Keep it basic and to the point. Let the money talk. Here's an example:

Dear Naomi: On the Pulling matter, where your client ran the stop sign and was cited, you have the police reports, the medical bills and all the charts and records, and the claimants pay stub's and tax returns for the last two years. I think this is all the documentation on damages; if I have missed something, let me know. Given the circumstances, our client would accept $260,000 in exchange for a full release of your insured. We await your thoughts. Best, Gordon.

What else is needed? Here's a possible reply:

Gordon: With reference to the Pulling matter, the police report indicates that your client may have been exceeding the speed limit, which would introduce some element of comparative. Further, the medical bills were paid at the health insurance contract rate, substantially below the billing a rate. Under the *circumstances, the company has authorized me to offer you $110,000 for a full release. Please advise. Naomi.*

Gordon did not have to explain his theory of the case, or how he constructed his damage demand. Pointing to the documentation that contained the basis for these elements was more than sufficient; Naomi could tell from this exactly where Gordon was coming from. Naomi did not have to explain the Gordon what the consequences of speeding would be, nor did she have to hammer that comparative negligence reduced or eliminated the amount of damage. Pointing to the fact in the police report, without adjectives or bludgeoning rhetoric, was more than sufficient. Gordon knows exactly what all this meant from the defense standpoint.

The take away here is that in any written exchanges aimed at opposing counsel and intended as a step in a negotiation to value, less is always better. When the objective is to reach an agreement upon a hard money value, construct the bid carefully to deliver the message desired, then let the money talk – get out of the way.

Even the evaluation of winning and losing has different connotations depending upon one's viewpoint. To the litigator, winning is absolute, to the negotiator, it is relative. Consider this example. The trial is six or seven months off. Now, after a number of rounds the plaintiff's lawyer has dropped the plaintiff's demand to $175,000. The defense replies the last few exchanges have been to make baby steps to $135,000, where she now is indicating that the defendant's side is probably very close to being "all in." What is the plaintiff's lawyer to think?

If the lawyer is still in litigation mode, he may think, "Nonsense, the offer is an insult; the case is worth much more." He does not listen or pay any attention to *why* the defense appears to be shutting down at $135,000. He focuses only on his own evaluation, to the strong points of his own case, and to the high end of it at that. Maybe he puts $173,000 out, and sends the message that his client is also "almost" all in at this number.

The negotiator considers where the defense is coming from. How come the defense fussed around with such low numbers and why are they now saying that the final number is around

$135,000? What does he know about this case that plaintiff's counsel doesn't? In running over the case in his mind and considering what he has learned from the messages being sent, the negotiator might learn that the defense is putting a different spin on a witness's expected testimony that just might appeal to a jury, and also that there might be a problem with some evidence on damages – in objectively assessing this information, counsel believes the risk factors are affected, which leads to an adjustment in values a bit. The negotiator adjusts the verdict range in his own mind as maybe being closer to $150,000 rather than $160,000. The defense offer of $135,000 is appearing to look a little better in a different light.

The negotiator also considers the factor of time, and the time-value of money. The reality is that there are months to go before the case gets to trial and the jury actually returns its verdict. Assuming plaintiff wins a verdict then, with all the post-trial motions that will follow, it may be another four to six months before a final judgment is issued and the first chance would finally appear for the plaintiff to receive any money – and even then, that would only be if the other side does not appeal. Plus it will cost a healthy sum for expert fees and other costs from this point forward to go to trial, which will have to be paid currently as they are incurred. Plaintiff will get some of these costs back if he wins, but probably not all, and nobody will know exactly how much will be recovered until the very end.

In a most important step, the negotiator will share all this with the client to determine what is more important – a net recovery today based upon something in the range of the $135,000 figure, which would be a sum certain that he can have in a week, or an expected net recovery on a potentially much higher sum, which he would not receive for at least a year, but with greater costs and greater risks involved? Counsel may be surprised to learn that the immediate cash obtained quickly is much more valuable to the client than the chance of a greater but considerably more remote jury verdict not expected for at least another year.

So with all this analysis, instead of stiffening up and returning with a demand in the higher range, the negotiator might meet the $135,000 offer with a reply demand of $155,000 or even

$150,000 – truly testing the message that the defendant was all in with an unmistakable invitation to split the difference, and with directions from the client to not let the settlement get away in any event.

Essence of the negotiator

The point here is that the litigator whose head is stuck in the trial mode can get locked into a "win at any cost" mind-set and fail to be objective about all the alternatives available. The lawyer who can shift into the negotiator mode is constantly evaluating the deal to keep in perspective the other side's position, its impact on value and risk, and the client's interests and concerns.

This mental shifting of gears can be difficult upon both lawyer and client. The client may find it confusing to read the lawyer's loyalty and dedication to the cause if he comes upon his lawyer in a reflective mood, attempting a collaborative examination of the opposing case in preparation for settlement discussions with opposing counsel.

Communication with the client is always important, but it becomes especially essential during any periods of transition, where the lawyer is transitioning back and forth between the position of a trial advocate preparing the arguments for the courtroom and that of a settlement negotiator preparing for discussion with the opposition. The lawyer must keep his client informed during these times of exactly where his head is at and why.

In summary, the trial attorney who can transition into a successful deal negotiator will do so in three critical areas:

- first is the ability to make a brutally frank and objective assessment of the entirety of the case including the weak points of his case and all of the opposition's strong points, all placed in perspective;
- second is the ability to engage in a frank and in depth explanation of all of these elements to the client – the bad parts with the good together with a practical discussion of

the client's best and worst and probable case outcomes; and

- third, is the ability to develop and maintain a friendly or at least neutral attitude towards the opposition generally – the case, the people and their lawyers – and maintain a level of cordiality in all communications and confrontations.

The lawyers who can reliably get themselves into this frame of mind whenever necessary to the effort can get their heads where they need to be for the rigors of a settlement effort; all that is necessary then is to work on the techniques.

Nothing in here says that anybody has to become a doormat or a marshmallow. It is much easier, of course, if the other side reciprocates in all of these areas, and is equally demonstrative about seeking a fair negotiated resolution. But the negotiation strategies will still work even where other side remains aloof, or hostile or even aggressive. Distributive negotiation is a competitive process, and the actual moves may be just as tough and concessions may be just as difficult to release as the circumstances of litigation will allow.

If counsel is not already one of the lawyers who are naturally in the frame of mind required, or cannot comfortably accommodate this transition required to get there, then the decision to rely upon mediation almost makes itself. Mediation will obviate most of the problem areas outlined above, and leave counsel alone in his adversarial mind set.

What counsel must remember here is that in any settlement effort, the money is the message, and that message has to be same whether delivered by a hand in a velvet glove or with a mailed fist.

4
Matters of principle and the economic rule

Before any discussion of settlement can occur, or any preparations for discussions of settlement, lead counsel must determine whether the case is amenable to settlement at all. This question will arise anytime liability is in dispute, where any of the disputed issues of liability turn on an issue of principle. If a matter of principle is involved, counsel must determine with the client whether the case is to be pursued as a matter of principle or whether it can be approached strictly as a matter of economics.

The overwhelming number of civil cases are resolved on the basis of pure economics, not upon principle. The settlement value of the case is determined exclusively by consideration of economic factors – resource, risk and cost – what can be won or lost in terms of money. The resolution on the basis of economics does not involve any element of truth, right, fairness, or justice. It is always the ice cold application of the economic rule: resource, risk and cost.

On the other hand, our system is also designed for the pursuit of justice on matters of principle, and there is nothing wrong with litigating an issue as a matter of principle. But there is a hard rule here: If the dispute to be litigated involves a matter of principle, it cannot be settled.

The reasons for this is definitional: To compromise a matter of principle is to abandon it, and since settlements invariably involve compromise, settling the case would amount to abandoning the matter of principle. This means that whenever a core issue pertaining to a matter of principle important to the client is disputed, the client must decide whether the case is to be pursued as a matter of principle, no matter what the cost, or whether counsel may pursue settlement upon an economic bases, accepting that no answer on the issue of principle will be obtained.

One cannot have it both ways. It cannot be “sort of” over principle and “mostly” just about the money, for by definition, one cannot “sort of” settle a matter of principle. So long as the client understands this, and understands the risks, and can afford the consequences of an adverse result, there is no basis for criticism on any insistence on going to trial over matters of principle. It is not a reflection upon anyone’s intelligence, wisdom or common sense to insist upon a trial where a matter of principle is at the core. Our entire system of justice is based upon access to the judicial system being available for just such tasks.

On the other hand, the vast majority of single action, one-off civil litigation lawsuits, whether involving matters of principle at their inception or not, are eventually resolved strictly upon the basis of economics. Most lawyers, and most clients after being exposed to the cost, the delays, the vagaries of jury verdicts, and the uncertainties of the process, recognize that single action, one-off litigation is too expensive and too uncertain to maintain strictly over matters of principle. But this decision must be made by the client, and it is imperative that the client understand the question involved and make the decision at the earliest practical time.

This means that when the client agrees to go forward with the settlement effort on the questionable outcome case, if the case is settled, it will be settled on the basis of pure economics. The final result will be derived from an objective consideration by both sides of the dollar evaluation of how much can be won (or lost), what the chances are of achieving that goal of winning (or losing), and what it's going to cost to find out.

There is not one iota of any of the elements of truth, right, justice, fairness, equity, individual responsibility or retribution in the determination of the case under the economic rule – it is the ice-cold analysis of the economics of the case, without regard to merit, need or entitlement. Where the mutual evaluation of risk is anywhere in the middle, the final settlement figure will necessarily reflect a substantial compromise by both sides from their base positions on this issue. This will not serve to declare who is right and who is wrong as a matter of principle, but will simply assign a dollar figure based upon the economic odds to end the case. Compromise settlements do not reach issues of principle.

Most business people – including insurers – are comfortable with this result. The economic considerations of resource, risk and cost are exactly the same considerations a businessman uses in making any ordinary business investment decision. The business person is aware that the economic formula does not address matters of principle, and is content to deal with these issues elsewhere. So long as the litigation client can be satisfied with this same approach, the lawyers can quantify and value the case exclusively upon consideration of the economic risks involved, drive to settle the case within the range of these considerations, strive to obtain the best settlement available within the parameters of the economic rule, and move on.

Of course, counsel may plan to argue issues of principle to the court and jury if the case goes to trial, but these arguments will have very little persuasive weight with the adversary during settlement negotiations. The practical result of obtaining the client's waiver of any objection over compromising an issue of principle is that counsel may redact all aspects of arguments over principle from any materials provided to the mediator and in all communications with the adversary.

And when negotiating directly or in a mediation – leave the soap box at home.

5
Administrative details: People, place and time

In a direct negotiation, only the attorneys will be involved – usually alone, sometimes on the telephone, and only sometimes with the clients present. Usually it is an advantage to separate the representative negotiators from the principals in direct negotiation, so the representatives can break the action to confer with the principals. In any event, the only individuals directly involved will be the lawyers and the clients.

In a mediation, however, where the process already involves a go-between, and everybody interested in the case is going to assemble in a single conference, the question of exactly who is going to attend becomes important.

Where the case involves individuals as parties, all the individuals with a stake in the outcome and entitled to a vote on the matter should show up for the mediation. Occasionally, in the case of a husband and wife, only one will want to attend, for in some couples, one is more comfortable with these kinds of decisions and the other is truly not needed. This is not a chauvinistic comment, for increasingly in the author's experience, it is the wife that shows up to hammer out the deal and not hubby. If there is even a suspicion that this is not the case, counsel needs to independently verify the arrangement with the intended absent spouse, to ensure that he or she truly does not want to attend and is completely at ease with the other spouse handling the whole thing. Counsel does not want to learn at midnight on the day of mediation, when papa announces that he needs to call mama for permission to sign the deal that has taken all day and into the night to work out, that mama's approval is necessary and she should have been at the conference after all.

Example: *the subcontractor appeared at the mediation with his lawyer in a construction dispute with a general contractor. He explained that his wife was the co-owner of their company, but they had decided she did not need to attend the mediation. He was the president, he explained, and she was just the secretary-treasurer. When the negotiation finally reached a deal close to midnight, the subcontractor suddenly got cold feet and decided that he better check with his wife before signing off on it. Of course, she balked, he would not sign, the deal did not go through that night, and it took the lawyers three more weeks to put it back together.*

When it was all wrapped up, the lawyers and the mediator concurred that as soon as the fellow said that his wife was going to stay home because she was "just" the secretary-treasurer, they should have known better.

Often, the problem is not in deciding who needs to attend, it is in keeping those who are not needed away. When the ones who have to be there want to bring along friends, siblings, family members, or anyone else, this can pose problems. It is one thing if the hangers-on on are just there to entertain and provide moral support; it is quite another if they expect to be allowed to put their oars in the water and help row the boat.

Example: *the claimant was a young adult, and had been injured in a two-car auto accident. She was a passenger in the vehicle being driven by her boyfriend, and, while she was free of any comparative negligence, the apportionment of negligence between the boyfriend and other driver was a significant issue. The mediation involved only the other driver, with the claim against the boyfriend's insurance carrier to be resolved at another time.*

At the mediation, the claimant and her lawyer showed up with (a) her boyfriend and (b) her mother. Opposing counsel pitched a fit over the boyfriend being in the room, and insisted that the boyfriend could not participate or be present at all, since he was an adverse party and his case was still pending. They had no objection, however, to the mom. So, the boyfriend was run off, and the mediation proceeded without him. What plaintiff's counsel did not know was that the boyfriend's presence was going to be needed to support the girl in facing up to her mom. The mom had just invited herself to the mediation. She knew nothing of the legal problems, and had not been part of the workup of the case. But she claimed she had a friend who had a friend who "knew about these things," and she was determined to make sure that her little girl was not taken advantage of by anybody.

It turned out the friend's friend was a transaction lawyer from another state who knew very little about personal injury cases, less about such cases in Idaho, and nothing about the case at hand, but nevertheless had plenty of opinions. Mom could not get it through her head that the offers were only for the adverse driver's share of the fault, not for the whole thing. The daughter, who was the actual claimant, understood all this. But as it was, the daughter was not able to stand up to the mom's furor, the boyfriend was not there to back her up, the claimant's lawyer could not get the mom to listen to reason, and eventually the mediation collapsed into a complete debacle. The mom insisted that they take the case elsewhere, so the lawyer withdrew. The boyfriend ran for cover. The mom could not find anyone to even look at the case let alone take it over. The girl finally talked the lawyer into coming back into the case as long as the mother was not involved, and it finally got settled. The girl did, however, lose her boyfriend in the process.

There is no question that having too many cooks in the kitchen is not wise. It might appear that the rule should be only the individuals involved in the loss can participate – but this can pose problems, too. Many times, having a parent or a significant other along can be helpful, or even necessary, even though the claimant may be an adult.

Example*: the case involved damages for discrimination in the handling of an adoption. The claimant was gay, and her process to adopt a child had been hopelessly mangled by an officiously biased and bigoted state bureaucrat. The mistakes had come late in the process, and the claimant was devastated by the loss. Because of the actions of the state, there was no way to put it right, and the only question was one of money damages. The state, through a risk manager, was anxious to get the case settled, and was working hard to make realistic offers. The claimant simply could not come to a decision. She was in tears most of the time, inconsolable from her attorneys and unwilling to accept any of the offers made by the state.*

Finally, the mediation was abandoned. On his way out of the building, the mediator noticed that the claimant had joined a woman who had been in the waiting room, and that both were quite upset. In a follow-up telephone conversation with claimant's counsel the mediator learned that the woman in the waiting room was the claimant's life partner. They were not married, but had been in a committed relationship for many years, and the woman was going to help co-parent the adopted child, if it could ever be arranged.

The mediator and the lawyer discussed whether the partner should have been included in the negotiations. The lawyer called back and said that he had talked with his client, and she very much thought that if her partner could be there, it would help. The mediation was quickly rescheduled, and restarted from where it left off. The claimant and her partner worked with their lawyer and the mediator. The claimant was still obviously upset at the whole thing, but with her partner nearby she was able to work through the process and a satisfactory result was quickly reached. It would not have happened without the couple being able to work together.

Where extra people are going to show up, it is imperative that counsel make sure that it is the client that wants the support of the additional player, and that the person is not just assuming a right to step in and take over. This is a special problem with young adult clients and their parents, and with elderly clients and their adult children. Sometimes having the support present is crucial; other times, the client may be perfectly capable of handling matters themselves. Counsel needs to be sensitive to the difference here.

Then, if extra people are going to join the team, this should be planned in advance, and counsel should insist that whoever is to attend the settlement conference expecting to say anything and be listened to must also attend the work sessions with lawyer and client getting ready for the negotiating sessions. These are the sessions when the lawyer expects to go over all the risk factors and work out the strategies with the client, make sure that the client is not still up in the clouds but has at least one foot firmly planted on earth, and understands the mechanics of the settlement process. As can be seen in some of the examples above, it can truly be deadly if the supporting cast has not been privy to these conversations early on, arrives at the negotiating session cold and then begins throwing their weight around.

Sometimes the extra participant does not even have to be in the room to be a problem. What can be especially troublesome is the situation where the client suddenly expresses a need to consult with someone by telephone – the mother who decides to bring her adult son up to speed, or the daughter who suddenly needs her father's permission to make the deal. Usually, counsel knows his clients well enough that he is prepared for this eventuality. The wife who is not planning on attending the mediation has been brought in for all the prep sessions, and is fully familiar with the going-in strategy of the mediation. Several calls have been made to her as the mediation moves along to keep her generally up to speed. The lawyer is satisfied that, as long as the wife does not feel she is being blind-sided, she will be comfortable with whatever the husband works out, but she does need to be kept informed.

On the other hand, it can go badly, too. The girl who suddenly needed her father's permission had promised her lawyer that this was not going to happen. She was perfectly capable of making up her own mind, and did not need her father's permission. But when it came time to actually make the decision, she caved. She could not do it without her father's blessing. The problem was that the father was a retired lawyer from another state, and he had some definite ideas on the value of the case to his little girl. The mid-conference telephone call to the father turned out to be a disaster. The father did not agree with anything that had happened, the girl clammed up and would no longer do anything requested of her, and the mediator had no option but to terminate the mediation. The lawyer was unable to get either father or client to work with him, and the case finally went to trial. The verdict was as predicted. The defendant's counsel had made an offer of judgment for an amount that would have been reached at the settlement conference, and which turned out to be a few dollars more than the verdict. As a result, the plaintiff lost most of her trial costs and had some of the defense costs assessed against them. The result was a final judgment that was considerably less than what would have been achieved at the mediation.

The take away here is for the lawyer to be sure he has explored with his clients all the possible ramification of the decision process. If the clients are the least bit uncomfortable making the decisions that have to be made alone, that the lawyer knows who else should or needs to be involved in the process. Finally, if there are to be any other voices that need to be consulted, whether at the conference or by telephone, the lawyer must ensure that all persons involved are included in the preparation and kept informed as appropriate during the negotiations.

Subrogation interests

Many claims include claims of others that must be included in the disbursal of any settlement. Typical are the subrogated claims of workers' compensation sureties, health insurance carriers and the claimant's private auto carrier for amounts paid on property damage and voluntary medical pay coverage. Where these interests exist, and where they are not already represented in the litigation, wise counsel will contact the entities before any consideration of settlement and explore the possibilities of getting the subrogated interests to share the risk with the injured party in any compromise by making some appropriate accommodations.

In difficult cases, the subrogated interests can be asked to participate in the lawsuit, to contribute costs, and to physically participate in the settlement effort. Where the subrogation interest is smaller, the outside entities can be asked to stay out of the way and allow plaintiff's counsel to handle all interests, but to agree to participate in the risk by agreeing to compromise the dollar amount of their claim on a pro rata or other appropriate basis, to include accepting a reduction for the allowance of fees.

The point here is to get all of the potential subrogation interests under control early, before any settlement is actually in hand or pending, and obtain at least an agreement in principle to share the risk. The subrogated carrier will be much more resistant to any accommodations if counsel waits until the money is already in hand or committed before trying to make deals down the line. Further, counsel will actually have no idea how to evaluate his client's actual interest in any settlement that is proposed until and unless he has reached an appropriate accord with the subrogated interests

The take away here is to get it done early.

Government and business entities

Getting the right corporate or government representatives to a mediation can be tricky. In small companies, the owners usually show up and there is seldom any question over their authority to settle. In larger companies, a strange assortment of individuals can appear.

The definition of who needs to be at the conference for a business entity usually appears in the mediator's materials as something like this:

"The representative at conference for a business or government entity will be an executive decision maker of the entity who will be fully familiar with the file and who will have full and sufficient personal authority to authorize settlement of the case. It is not sufficient if the representative at conference is only a messenger or delegate who must report to and seek instructions from someone else."

However it is defined, the executive officer with decision making authority over the specific budget within the company that is going to take the hit for the consequences of the litigation should be the one selected to attend the mediation sessions and speak on behalf of the company.

The decision maker at a mediation conference over any serious litigated matter should be a line officer and not staff; the task should not be delegated to a support executive unless the litigation is routine to the enterprise and the representative assigned is the individual normally tasked to handle the issues. The decision maker can bring staff support as needed, but the person whose neck is on the line needs to be the one attending the conference and directly calling the shots. If the individual's authority is not obvious from his or her position and title, it should be confirmed with the CEO or general counsel, with any limitations clearly expressed.

What is not acceptable is for the person just described to stay in his office and have a staffer show up with only "first round" authority. This means they have authority to make the offer that has essentially already been turned down, but then they must call and get instructions for every subsequent move. Usually, the person they are calling is the decision maker who should be at the conference in the first place.

The executive who insists on staying behind his own desk and sending a delegate to appear in person may have good intentions, and may do his best to be quickly available at the beginning. But invariably, he will have other things to do, and it will become increasingly difficult to get him on the phone. As the day wears on, towards the end, there will inevitably be a development in the negotiation making it essential to get a fast answer to a current move. Murphy's Law says that the more important the case, the greater the likelihood that the guy who has to make the decision will be nowhere to be found.

If the cost of the mediator plus the hourly rate of all the lawyers plus a fair sum for the time of the other participants is added up, even a modest mediation will easily soak up $10,000 per day in total. If it is a high powered case with teams of lawyers on both sides and one of the top drawer mediators, the cost can easily approach $20,000 just for the day – not counting the time taken to prepare. There is really very little excuse for an executive necessary to the effort to claim that his or her time is more valuable, and attempt to work the process with a puppet. The failure of one side to meet the requirements of the mediation is grounds for the other side to call the process off at the gate. Most mediators will not proceed unless the opposing side waives the failed condition and consents to proceed. Those sophisticated with the process may not do so.

Not only that, but it risks the wrath of the court and offers the potential for severe sanctions.

Example: *A case the author was retained to mediate involved a number of plaintiffs who were injured in an industrial accident at a major employer's site in Idaho. An alarm system that was recently installed and under warranty failed to go off, resulting in a number of employees being caught unaware of a catastrophic equipment malfunction. The result was several deaths and a number of very serious injuries. The liability appeared fairly clear, with the only real question being the amount of damages. The expectation of all involved was that the settlement value of the case was going to be in the seven, perhaps even eight figure range. The mediation was scheduled at the location of the federal court in another city, which required everyone to travel. When the mediation started, a single lawyer from the defendant's trial team showed up with an assistant general counsel of the named defendant company. The company itself was fully insured for the loss, but no one from the insurance carrier was present. The defendant's lawyer explained that the regional claims manager was available by telephone. When asked if he or the assistant general counsel from the defendant company had any authority themselves to make any settlement offers, he said no – all authority had to come from the insurance company. When asked if either even had first round authority, and the answer was no, that the defense lawyer had been instructed to call to obtain authority before making any offers in the case at all.*

This was directly contrary to the terms of the mediation agreement, which provided that if there was insurance, a claims executive from the insurance company with personal authority sufficient to settle the case was to be physically present at the conference. The plaintiffs refused to proceed, and the conference adjourned at the gate.

Plaintiff's counsel immediately moved the court for sanctions. After an extensive hearing, the court entered a blistering order finding the defense insurance carrier had acted in bad faith. He awarded travel costs to all the plaintiffs, and travel costs and attorney fees to the plaintiffs' lawyers.

It is up to the lawyers to learn enough about their client's organizational structure and the personality of the individuals responsible for each so they can clearly determine who needs to be at the conference. Then they must make it happen.

Participation by telephone

The next worst thing to the executive staying behind and trying to run a mediation through puppets is the executive who wants to stay behind and participate by telephone. This is usually a bad idea, and is usually against the conditions established by competent mediators.

Mediation is a process, and it requires the individual participation of both sides to reach maximum effect. It is not fair for one party to participate the process while the other party is allowed to remain insulated by staying behind, connected only by telephone.

That said, this practice is nonetheless growing in favor in several specific areas of mediation and so it cannot be dismissed out of hand. It usually involves an insurance company and is an outgrowth of their emerging practice to assign high profile cases to specific claims specialists who are knowledgeable about the type of case rather than to general adjusters from the local area of the loss. These claims specialists may be located anywhere in the country, as they handle nothing but a particular type of case. Unless the potential liability is huge, they work exclusively by telephone and electronic mail. While these claims specialists routinely show up where needed for very large claims, it is not uncommon for them to want to handle what they may consider more routine claims by telephone. If all the metrics are in place, it can work.

A second category of insurance cases that also insists upon having the adjuster participate by telephone are the much smaller cases where a line adjuster has been handling the entire claim by telephone. There are a number of companies that are going entirely to telephone adjusters rather than local adjusters. The telephone claims department may be anywhere. It is virtually impossible to get these telephone adjusters to personally attend the mediation. If they are not allowed to participate by telephone, the company will engage an independent adjuster from the area to sit in at the mediation, who will have no authority other than to represent that they are attending to settle the case. They say nothing in the presence of the mediator, and insist on meeting in private with the defense lawyer before every round. In reality the whole thing is being run by the company adjuster on the telephone. From a practical standpoint, one might as well accept the telephone adjuster's participation, rather than the independent adjuster, if for no other reason than the ability to have the mediator actually talk directly to the line adjuster if need be.

Telephone participation by either the claims specialist for the high profile case or a telephone line adjuster for the more mundane type case may be acceptable if all four of these particular conditions exist:

- The representative was (a) assigned this case because of the individual's special expertise in cases of this type, or (b) was assigned this as a routine matter of course for telephone adjusting in general, and in both cases, it is the individual representative's routine practice to handle all cases of this sort by telephone; and the representative has experience or training in mediation conferences by telephone.
- The case is of a type routinely encountered by the company and routinely handled by telephone; it is not a one-off, a "bet the company" case, a case with unique public relations problems, a case intended as a test case

for any aspect, or a case with special risk factors that might turn it into a runaway; and

- Counsel who appears for the defending party in the mediation is an experienced insurance defense litigator with either (a) personal experience with this representative or (b) personal experience with telephone mediation or (c) both; and
- There is not some special reason that is unique to this litigation and necessitates the physical presence of the decision maker, such as would prevent opposing counsel from approving a reasonable request.

In these very specialized or very routine cases, the insurance representatives become immune to the impact of the settlement process. While this process may be important to the claimant, who is not familiar with business end of settling cases, the insurance representatives are very familiar and nothing is really lost in the effort by allowing these types of claims to be handled by telephone.

Notwithstanding these exceptions, the general rule should still be to require all parties to attend and participate in person.

The right person with authority

If the individual within the company who was responsible for getting the company into the pickle giving rise to the lawsuit in the first place then turns up as the head of the evaluation team to negotiate a solution, things can get awkward. As the mediation progresses through the day, the examination is going to touch on the actions and non-actions of everyone responsible for the occurrence – which means this fellow's shoes are going to pinch. Sometimes this is unavoidable, in small companies with close management for example, but if it can be avoided, the individual with decision making authority over settlement of the lawsuit should be someone who can objectively assess the risks without having to consider his own participation in it. If the company is big enough, and the management is diverse enough, the executive assessing the risk of the lawsuit should not be the same person who caused it in the first place.

Example: *in a bad faith case against a health insurance company for mishandling a first party health insurance claim, the breach of contract/tort case against the company was initially administered by the claims unit that had been handling the underlying health claim where the practices that were alleged to be the basis of the bad faith action arose. The company was treating the bad faith claim as an extension of the health claim under the policy. The supervisor of the claims unit appeared at the mediation.*

Within the first two hours, it became apparent that the employees of the company who were at the core of the bad faith claim were the employees of his unit – and that circumstances would probably reach him, too, since he was supervisor over all major decisions. For some reason, this had escaped everyone's attention until the mediation. The rep called the company's general counsel who recommended that the mediation recess, the claim file for the bad faith claim be reassigned within the company to a unit with a different reporting chain, and then the mediation could be reconvened when the new claims unit was up to speed.

The recommendation was followed, and a new supervisor was brought into the picture. Within a week or so, this new claims supervisor undertook settlement efforts directly with claimant's attorney, and was able to settle the case to the claimant's satisfaction without reconvening the mediation.

A second type of problem to avoid if possible is when the case involves issues of contract and the transaction lawyer who drafted the original contract shows up at the mediation to "help." In this day of modern litigation, it is the rare case where the lawyer who represented the client in the formation of the contract should represent the client in litigation over the enforcement of it if there is any issue over the validity of the contract. Although it is more subtle, exactly the same problems can arise if the transactional work was handled by another lawyer from the same firm. It is not a conflict of interest requiring referral of the case, or the erection of any Chinese walls, it is sufficient if the transactional lawyer just stays out of the trial team's hair. Usually, all problems can be avoided by making sure that the litigation is handled by a different lawyer in the firm, which will probably work unless the transaction lawyer wants to stay involved to "help."

As a general rule, trial counsel should probably not include the transaction lawyer as part of the trial team for any purpose. If the transaction lawyer is going to be a witness in the case over any issue other than pure ministerial identification of documents and confirmation of who signed what, or anytime the underlying contract itself is going to be at issue, the transactional lawyer is going to be in the way when it comes time to objectively assess the risks. Human nature being what it is, that lawyer is going to become defensive over his work and may well turn into an obstacle. Further, in trying to keep the shiny side up and his fanny out of the fire, he might say the wrong thing at the wrong time and inadvertently provide a verbal hand grenade to the other side. If there is going to be any question over the interpretation of the contract, the last person trial counsel will want wandering around off leash and un-muzzled is the original draftsman of the problem document.

Not too many cooks in the kitchen

Finally, especially when representing a governmental entity, it is important to avoid having too many representatives at the mediation. Experience teaches that the probability of success at mediation involving the government is inversely proportional to the number of government employees attending the conference. It's just like mother teaches: too many cooks in the kitchen will spoil the soup.

Having too many participants is uniquely a government phenomenon. When a business entity is sued, it may send a platoon of lawyers into the fray, but rarely will authorize more company resources than are absolutely necessary. On the other hand, whenever a lawsuit looms to address an issue under some government agency's aegis, everyone with their fingerprints on the project expects to be in on the autopsy, and may well show up at any mediation.

Example: *In a major construction dispute following the completion of a large complex of buildings on campus, those involved included the state university, the state department of administration, the state attorney general's office, the architect, the general contractor and 24 subcontractors. The whole works wound up in court over the contractor's action against the state for equitable adjustment of its contract and all 24 subcontracts, essentially involving litigation over what the general contractor and its subcontractors considered to be adverse decisions on hundreds of change order requests. The court ordered everybody into mediation early in the case. The general contractor with a passel of his staff and his lawyers, and all the subcontractors with their lawyers showed up at the first meeting on the claimants' side. A team of attorneys from the attorney general's office plus over 25 state and university employees, the architect's with its lawyers, and some direct consultants turned up on the government's side. The initial meeting required an auditorium.*

Not much was going to happen with this many people clogging up the works. It was going to take multiple sessions anyway, but just to see what would happen, the mediator ran the first session well past 5:00 p.m. Over half the room bailed out promptly on the hour, and within the next hour, another quarter of the participants drifted away.

The mediation stretched over five sessions and took almost 18 months to complete. During the first hiatus, the general contractor organized all the subcontractors and urged them all to stand down and allow the general contractor to manage the claim against the state defendants on their behalf. All the subs were on the job through his general contract anyway, and although they could pursue their claims individually, all the claims were derivative and dependent upon the general contract. Every one of the subcontractors agreed, reducing the claimant in numbers down to the general contractor and his lawyers. From a negotiating standpoint, the strength of the general's hand was immeasurably stronger, since he now held all the claims – there was no way for the state to divide up the opposition, and pick off individual subcontractor claimants one at a time.

On the state's side, fewer and fewer individuals showed up for each of the follow-up sessions. The true decision makers for the defense side were the financial folks from the university and the project manager from the state department of administration. Everyone else were just on-lookers, curious to see how it was going to turn out. The few people with technical information necessary to the financial decisions had already been extensively interviewed, and the financial people were fully informed with what they needed to know.

The whole matter was finally resolved in a session that ran close to midnight, and involved the general contractor and his counsel on one side, and three people from the government plus their lawyers on the other. For this final push, the general left his project superintendent and the on-site manager behind and ran the thing himself with his lawyer. The state finally worked itself down to the vice president of finance from the university, and the bureau chief and project manager from the public works department of the state, plus the state's lawyers.

Whether it would have gone any faster if this group had been in control from the beginning is problematic; the process required that everybody at least have the opportunity to participate.

But what is apparent here is that where a very large group starts out on either or both sides, it is important to winnow that group down to the fewest of essential individuals as quickly as possible.

From the standpoint of counsel's planning, what is needed to represent a business or governmental agency at a mediation is an individual or group of individuals to fulfill the following functions, *and no more*:

- a decision maker for the entity, *not a messenger,* who should have personal or delegated authority to run the show and should be the highest ranking individual within the company who has line authority to make operating decisions at least up to that needed to settle the case; and

- an individual (or individuals – the fewest number feasible) who has or have working knowledge of the facts underlying the disputes, who can assist the decision maker in objectively assessing how the occurrence in suit complies with the normal operating expectations of the company; and
- an individual who is familiar with the financial operations of the entity and who either has authority to implement, or can advise the decision maker on implementation, of the financial requirements of any settlement reached.

If these functions can be combined in one person, great; more likely, it will be a team, but it should be the smallest team that can be assembled to fully cover the required bases. The point to take away here is to streamline and shorten the decision making process to its absolute essential.

Witnesses or select experts

Occasionally, someone will indicate that they will bring a key witness or an expert to the mediation, in case there are any questions.

If someone on the mediation team needs the witness to attend and consult, there is no problem. In a recent case in the author's experience, the parties' outside accountant attended; but she was needed to help the parties and their counsel work through the damage calculations. She did not participate in the decision making, nor have any discussion separately with the mediator, but was just a consultant.

What may pose problems is when it is announced that the extra individual is there to convince the opposition or the mediator on the party's position. This is universally a waste of time.

The mediator is not deciding anything, and does not need to be persuaded on the intricacies of the technology. There is no point in trying to persuade him of anything. Even if he is a retired judge, he is not the judge of this case, and will stay away from attempting to judge this case. He is there only to assist in the process of negotiation. All the mediator needs is sufficient understanding of the technology to see where the issues are, and to guide the parties in addressing them. He can get everything he needs from the lawyer's explanations, he does not need anything from the expert.

As to a witness at the mediation persuading the opposition of anything, this is simply not going to happen. It does not matter what the expert's credentials are, how thorough his research has been, or how solid his opinions appear to be. The other side is not going to be impressed by anything he has to say at mediation. Assuming they are well prepared, they will have digested the expert's work as part of their preparation, keeping it in perspective with their own expert's opinions and the other evidence in the case. It is a waste of time and money to bring fact witnesses or experts to a mediation conference with the expectation that they will impress the other side with anything.

Selecting the location

This is not a consideration in direct negotiation, for it will occur wherever the negotiators happen to be – in each other's offices or more likely, over the telephone.

It *is* a consideration in a mediation.

Early on, there was an insistence that these things be conducted in neutral territory. Lawyers, parties and mediators traipsed off to all manner of places – courthouses, hotel conference centers, churches, and school auditoriums – any place that could be found. Brief meetings on folding chairs and card tables in the basement of the courthouse or church may be OK for any civic or community functions, but sustaining a 10 hour mediation under such conditions can become excruciating.

As the lawyers' comfort level with the process of mediation increased, the need for neutral territory declined. The expense of hotel space and the insistence that courthouse facilities had to vacate promptly at 5:00 p.m. chafed. This and the lack of creature-comfort considerations found in too many of the make-do facilities found elsewhere eventually drove everybody back into their own offices.

Today, most firms include conference space set up for mediation. Most office buildings that cater to lawyers have extra conference space available. The question no longer is over neutral territory, but rather over whose place.

The decision here should turn exclusively on creature comfort considerations. Figure the conference to be long. In terms of having to spend all day and into the evening in the facility, who has the better set up in terms of parking, access, wi-fi available, decent size rooms, comfortable chairs, and windows with a view? Perhaps decent, nearby restaurants if the conference is to break for lunch or decent carry-out that delivers if not. If one location over others does not clearly emerge from consideration of these elements, then flip a coin.

On timing the settlement effort

A major strategy decision that must be made early on is, when is the case going to be ready for a settlement effort?

The smart aleck answer is, "When it's ripe." This functionally useless answer is nevertheless correct. The problem is that every case ripens at a different time, and it becomes a matter of judgment to determine the appropriate time. Some cases are ready for settlement before the complaint is even filed. Other cases need at least the claimant's deposition. Still others may require all the discovery including experts to be completed. How much is enough? It depends.

The key to success in settlements is the same as the key to success in trials: preparation. Knowledge is power but preparation is king. The importance of preparation cannot be over emphasized. Lack of preparation is probably the most significant reason for failure in settlement efforts.

The lodestar ideal of preparation required for any serious effort at settlement is to have the case prepared as if going to trial, meaning thorough preparation on essential elements to the degree expected for trial. One must expect that the opponent in the settlement effort will be fully aware of every single weakness in the case, whether it has been revealed or not, and counsel must be prepared to handle that eventuality.

The basic due diligence, independent investigation of facts, verification of documents and other tangible things, and updating of all legal research that the trial lawyer will demand of himself before going into the trial, would be a minimum. Appropriate assurance that all written discovery is in hand and complete, perhaps the deposition of the opposing party and key opposition witnesses, perhaps adverse expert reports or their deposition. The list goes on. In fairness, trial attorneys are never satisfied that their case is ready for trial until the Bailiff cuts them off on the first day of trial with the command to stand up for the court.

It is not necessary that every scrap of trial prep be completed before a settlement effort is attempted. Interview notes and experts reports maybe sufficient without requiring completed depositions. Basic discovery from the opposition should be in hand and digested, but without the extensive "batten down the hatches" scouring that may be conducted prior to trial. Depending upon the technology, expert reports may be unnecessary for settlement purposes; counsel can assume that the other side will have whatever experts they will need at trial, without actually seeing the completed work. Exhibit blowups, videos and animations, and other trial paraphernalia do not have to be completed. The plaintiff's deposition may be an essential, but the defense depo may be unnecessary.

In many other situations, where minimizing the mounting costs is a factor in settlement, it is not feasible to insist that trial prep be complete before discussions of settlement are begun. Then, the question of readiness will turn on counsel's own determination of how much is enough in order to support a decision on when to open negotiations. As long as the basic due-diligence has been completed, and counsel is thoroughly familiar with the file, it is a judgment call how far other preparation and discovery has to go before the case is ready for settlement efforts.

Early case evaluation and mediation is a settlement effort attempted very early, with only a minimal exchange of information and no more that the deposition of the parties. It can work with simple cases without labyrinthine legal theories. The more complicated or technical the case, the less likely an early evaluation will be acceptable. The key to most shortcut efforts is a careful stipulation of all assumptions and conditions applicable to the early event.

The best that can be said here is that under any circumstance, it should be at a point where the entire case can be assessed with confidence. There should be no open questions and there cannot be any major surprises in the fundamental details of the occurrence, in the facts or contentions of the parties, or in the legal theories and defenses that are involved.

Finally, and of paramount importance if any shortcut is to be employed, is for the client to understand and agree with the status of the case, tactical decisions that are being made, and the objectives being sought.

6
Client preparation

The aspect of separate client preparation for settlement is probably not necessary if the client has otherwise been kept closely informed about the case as it has proceeded into the settlement effort, and is already familiar with all the steps that have been taken to date. The critical problem this requirement is designed to avoid is to where there is any risk the client will learn of some feature of the case for the first time in the middle of settlement negotiations, or worse, at the mediation conference.

The evaluation process for any settlement requires the party to be realistic about recognizing the differing views of value, upon the fact that juries may differ as to values, and upon the economic realities of an immediate settlement versus the time expectations if the case is to go to a verdict. The process contemplates haggling as a recognized way of determining value, meaning compromises on monetary value may be expected. Unless the client is unusually stubborn, these compromises are nothing more than recognition of life's differences and should require little in the way of preliminary coaching.

But it is absolutely essential that the client be up to speed on all of these aspects before there are any direct negotiations, and that the client is not still lost in the clouds over the prospects of his case in the middle of any mediation conferences. If the case is one where liability has been admitted, and the damages only are at issue, the client must understand that the record-breaking damage award he read about online is irrelevant; the predicted settlement value is going to be a more plebeian value derived from counsel's estimates of average verdicts. If the client will only truly be satisfied with a verdict that reaches the fences, he is going to have to get that from a jury – and take the risk.

Where liability is at issue and any settlement will probably be at a figure that recognizes the risk and compromises the value, this must be thoroughly understood by the client. The issue of waiving litigation over matters of principle versus a settlement upon the economic realities of the circumstance must be understood and agreed upon. The client must be satisfied that the issues of principle will probably not be resolved in any settlement attained, and counsel must ensure that the client understands and agrees with this objective. It is vastly preferred that this be fully understood by the client before any settlement discussions with the adverse counsel are begun in earnest, and it must be agreed upon before any mediation.

If the first explanation to the client about the realities of a settling a case where there is any doubt about the outcome, and of the compromises on principles that must be accepted, comes after offers from the other side begin to flow at mediation, and counsel is faced with explaining for the first time why the adversary offers are where they are, counsel may find client management has suddenly become a much more daunting challenge than was anticipated.

The heart-to-heart discussion that must occur to satisfy this requirement will come much easier if the client has been kept fully informed on all aspects of the case as it progressed. If the client has been copied on all correspondence and pleadings, has attended all depositions and court hearings, or has received copies of transcripts and thorough reports of court proceedings, and has participated in all strategy sessions, then bringing the client to speed when counsel makes the determination that the case needs to be categorized as an in-betweener case from among the good/bad quadrants for settlement consideration purposes will be much easier.

Where the client resists the lawyer's explanations, things can get difficult. A typical scenario that may lead to this problem is when the lawyer was a little too effusive about the prospects of the case at the outset. If the clients have not been kept continuously in the loop as the case develops, witnessing for themselves the emergence of problem issues and difficult facts, and participating with the lawyer and his team in all the steps of case evaluation, then when the lawyer tries to bring the clients to speed on the issue of settlement, the lawyers may meet considerable resistance. Counsel may find that the clients have fastened on the lawyer's initial extravagance, elevated the words into promises, and now are unwilling to let go. "Yes, but you said ..." The clients keep repeating as counsel tries to explain the current posture of the case; "Yes, but you said ..."

First thing to do is keep at it. Keep explaining to the client, over and over as necessary, until it sinks in. Look for allies among others in the client's camp – the spouse, parents, adult children or siblings may be of help here, or other executives on the same or higher levels within the company, if the lawyer can get them to understand the problem and help turn the client. Where the client is the head of the family, or the CEO of the company, or is otherwise used to being in charge, seeking allies may not work, but where the client is other than the actual head of the operation, others may weigh in, and where you can get help, this can be immeasurably useful.

Another alternative is for the lawyer to call in another member of the law firm or, if practicing solo, a mentor to serve as a foil in a frank discussion about the case. In TV lingo, to play "good cop, bad cop," with the bad cop on clear orders not to cave in when the client repeats, "Yes, but you said..."

A final strategy is to use the mediator. Mediators are useful at delivering bad news to clients without any danger of being boxed in by the promises allegedly made at the outset.

It is necessary that counsel go over the ground with the client first, at least once and preferably more. If the client hears the bad news only from a stranger, the client may simply shut it out and ignore it. Instead, he should hear it one or two times from his own lawyers, then if it is not sinking in, the mediator can cover the same ground in context with the messages being delivered from the opposition.

It is essential to this strategy that the mediator be cued in advance as to what is expected. Sometimes, it is useful for the mediator, lawyers and clients to have a special session in advance of the regular mediation to go over these matters. The device of the clients hearing something from this mystical stranger from afar who the lawyers have called in to work some kind of magic, that is word for word what the lawyer had been saying all along, may provide a sort of epiphany or gestalt that works to jar the listener into realization.

The take-away point here is that the client must be on board with the fact that it is questionable outcome case, and with the objective of recognizing a compromise in order to reach an economic answer to get it settled. If the client insists on a resolution of issues of principle or for any reason cannot recognize the economic realities of the predicted settlement ranges for the case, any settlement will be out of reach until the client comes around.

7
Financial capacity

In the usual case, the financial capacity of either party to a lawsuit is legally irrelevant. Unless somehow directly relevant to a substantive issue in the suit, the lawyers are not obligated to reveal anything of their client's finances to the opponent in discovery, and the opponents are not legally entitled force the information from others until and unless a judgment is actually entered. Lawyers do not pry into their client's financial worth beyond satisfying themselves of the client's ability to pay the lawyer's fees on a current basis – and sometimes, they are not even very good at that. The law protects untoward inquiry into a party's financial affairs until there is a legal reason for the inquiry.

However, there are several areas of litigation where it can be very important to make a deeper inquiry into the financial condition, either of the client or of the opponent, notwithstanding the general rules and the technical relevancy of the matter. Consider first a situation where the lawyer's client has been sued in a hopeless case. He is going to be found liable, and the only question is by how much. A negotiated solution is always possible, where the parties agree upon the amount of damages sustained and thereby avoid the expense and inconvenience of the lawsuit.

In such a case, the prospect of an adverse verdict is a certainty rather than a possibility. The efforts of counsel would be directed in keeping the result to a manageable amount, and preventing a disaster. In such case, the financial capacity of the client to absorb the consequences may be material to the tactical considerations that the lawyer must make in negotiating the case.

If the client has capacity to handle an adverse judgment, the task for the defense is to strive for the least amount of damages attainable, based upon the facts of the case. However, if the situation is hopeless, and the client does not have the capacity to handle an adverse judgment, no matter how much it might be, the wisest course may be to steer the client towards a different solution altogether.

The point here is that by going forward with a mediation or entering into negotiations with the other side for determination of damages, there is at least some implication that the client will be able to perform if an agreement is reached. Where this is hopeless, it does not make any sense to go to the expense of negotiating a resolution of the breach based upon the amount owed if the client is not going to be able to perform anyway.

In such case, if the situation is truly hopeless, the client might best be convinced to throw in the towel. To seek protection in bankruptcy and call off the settlement efforts in current litigation.

If there is some room for performance, but nothing sufficient to the actual damages, the strategy might be to disclose the client's financial condition to the opposition, and work out a settlement based upon what the client can afford and is willing to pay to avoid the stigma of bankruptcy. Attempt to settle the case for an amount within range of what the client can actually handle, without regard to the actual values of the case.

Threading the needle here is by convincing the opponent that a fully valued deficiency judgment would prove uncollectable as it would only precipitate a bankruptcy; however, the client may be willing to pay some amount to avoid bankruptcy, but only if it solves the lawsuit. It is essential that the lawyer knows what the client's financial status is in order to plan a strategy to accommodate this kind of theory.

The take away point is that whenever the lawyer is taking on anything in the range of hopeless defense case, counsel needs to add a fourth element to the economic formula of resource, cost and risk, that being "capacity."

Where the prospects of a very large adverse judgment appear probable, beyond the capacity of the client to manage, other alternatives need to be considered. Any evaluation of the case based upon economic reality must include the capacity of the client to absorb or pay an adverse judgment in order to justify spending good money defending the case in the ordinary course.

If the expected adverse result is not within the client's capacity but there is some room for performance, it may be possible to attack the problem by presenting a reality based alternative directly to the opposition. The idea is to achieve a pragmatic settlement within the capacity of the defendant rather than force a bankruptcy. Counsel must demonstrate to the opposition that the client has no capacity to handle an adverse result if the opponent presses for a verdict or insists upon a settlement based upon what is actually owed.

The capacity defense, when properly presented, can work with a sophisticated business plaintiff. Business plaintiffs such as banks, credit unions, credit agencies and the like, usually have no interest pursuing a matter to judgment just for the paper behind it. If the defendant is or is going to be truly judgment proof and without prospects, but is willing to take on a modest amount to avoid the stigma of bankruptcy, some sophisticated plaintiffs will take what they can get, even if only a token, and call it a day. They realize that if they force the issue to judgment, whatever resources the defendant was willing to advance in the modest settlement will be used up or disappear into a protected asset before the bankruptcy is filed and there will be nothing left by the time any judgment issues.

For this tactic to work, it is essential that the party be completely honest and forthcoming in revealing his financial condition. He must expect that the any statements will be investigated, and any attempt at withholding information or concealing assets or resources will not only sabotage any chance at settlement, but will leave the party far worse off in the litigation than before. He will still have the losing lawsuit on his hands, but now with an opposing party who will have a roadmap to all his assets and resources. Counsel must emphasize upon his client that this is not the time to try to be cagey or coy in providing information or answering inquiries.

The exact same consideration can work in the reverse when the problem is on the other side. If your client has a strong case against an individual for damages of the zero sum nature –

meaning the object of the suit is not tied to any asset or tangible resource from which the amount due can be drawn, like an insurance policy, the question of whether the defendant has the capacity to pay any judgment becomes a real issue. Even in a contingent fee case, significant investment in litigation costs may be required which would be wasted if the defendant proves to be judgment proof. If, through the resources available, you determine that the individual probably does not have the capacity to respond should a judgment be entered, consideration should at least be given to broaching the subject of a capacity-measured settlement.

Finally, the best chances of success will come if this alternative from either side is pursued early, before the adverse party has incurred too much in the way of costs or fees and becomes, in effect, "pot committed" to see the case through to the end, even if it appears the result will be a worthless judgment.

8
Winners and losers and in-betweens

The most important decision counsel will make in the process may well be the decision that is made not to take the case in the first place. To say this another way, the decisions that probably save counsel the most money in the long run are the decisions made to decline representation.[1]

The potential case the client brings in to plaintiff's counsel for consideration of suit can be sorted in triage two different ways. Either by potential outcome: winner, loser or in between, or by amount in controversy: a lot, a little, or in-between. While counsel may want to say that they only intend to accept cases that are winners of potentially large verdicts, the practical situation make this almost impossible. Too often, counsel get tangled up with fascination over the potential for the amount of recovery without spending enough time or attention on the basic issue of whether recovery of anything is possible at all, or vice versa.

These are pragmatic divisions, not technical categories with sharply defined boundaries. The differences are in the element of risk assessment on outcome and value and in the element of

---

1 With many exceptions that are plainly noted, the parts on negotiation strategies are generally written from the viewpoint of a plaintiff or plaintiff's lawyer, meaning the one making the claim or starting the lawsuit and expecting to recover money from someone else. If the reader is one who has been sued, or is a lawyer who customarily represents defendants who have been sued, the methods, tactics and strategies analyzed here are exactly the same, but often applied in reverse. Although the mechanisms are the same, the degree to which they will apply, the impact of the risks involved and the results actually attained are seldom the exact obverse of those expected on the plaintiff's side. The defense chances in settlement prospects, as in general litigation, are not the flip side of the plaintiff's coin, but must be separately examined and analyzed for all the elements of value and risks involved, almost as though it were a different case.

control of the litigation processes. It may look simple, but each of the categories can present very tricky edges.

In the ideal world, losing cases would not be pursued at all, or if started would be dropped as soon as the true nature of the case is identified. Litigation is way too expensive to pursue a case to the bitter end once it becomes clear that there is no hope. Plus, in almost every jurisdiction, there are strong sanctions that the courts will impose upon both client and lawyer if the court perceives that a frivolous case is being pursued without foundation. This means there must at least be some good faith argument for the existence of facts or law under which the claiming party might prevail.

The problem is, the decision points are not precisely defined. It is not at all unusual for there to be considerable room to debate the predicted outcome or the predicted value of a given case, with the claiming party, for example, convinced that the case has a decent chance at winning a substantial verdict, while the defending party is equally convinced that it is nothing more than a barking dog. It is not going to be established whether the case was a winner or loser until the case is tried.

Also, there are cases which appear to have little or no chance of winning, yet are still considered worth pursuing. Included here are cases where the chance of winning may appear slight, but the verdict, if one is attained, will be huge. Also included here are the cases which are losers today, but which present a reasonable expectation of changing the law. So long as both client and counsel understand the actual probabilities, and have the wherewithal to finance the effort and absorb the risk, there is nothing wrong with pursuing such cases – such is the essence of our system of justice.

Cases against tobacco companies are an example of cases which appear hopeless but may produce huge paydays. Ever since reports linking cancer deaths to smoking came out in the 1950's, cases have been pouring into the courts brought by the families of deceased smokers suing tobacco companies. The tobacco companies prevailed in all of these early suits for over 30 years, until finally their armor was cracked in the 1980's. A few courts began to hold that certain cases involving certain facts could go to a jury. Suddenly, plaintiff's verdicts began to appear and slowly spread, and when they did appear, they were very large. These cases are still on very, very long odds, but the occasional verdicts that are being returned are huge, and are sufficient to keep the cases flowing. In 2014, a Florida jury awarded the widow of a former smoker $23 billion in damages against R. J. Reynolds. Although the appellate court then reduced the verdict to "only" $17 million, results like this are more than sufficient stimulus to keep these cases coming.

Settlement evaluation matrix

What is needed is a matrix of some kind, where any case under consideration can be spread out and placed in order to assess its relative position. When viewed from the plaintiff's side, every claim in litigation will fall somewhere within one of the quadrants here.

Good Facts-Good Law	**Good Facts-Bad Law**
Bad Facts-Good Law	**Bad Facts-Bad Law**

The contents of each quadrant of the opponent's box for each claim will be, by definition, the obverse of the content of the plaintiff's boxes. This means that upon an objective assessments of each claim, it is not logically possible for both sides to share the same quadrant. If a claim presents a case of "good facts/bad law" for the plaintiff, then by definition, it will be a case of "bad facts/good law" for the defense. If it appears that this is not so, if both sides appear to be claiming the "good facts/good law" quadrant on the same element of the case, then someone is wrong. In the simple case, this matrix would apply to the entire case. In more complex cases, each issue or count could be measured against its own matrix and scored, with the entire case measured by the scores of each part.

While the quantum of measurements may differ, the existence of the factor itself is fairly objective. What is a "good" fact or law for the plaintiff is a "bad" fact or law for the defense, and visa-versa, even though the quantitative measurement of how good or how bad the element is may be somewhat subjective. This means that when a case is properly developed, the opposing sides should be on the same page with regard to the allocation of basic factors, with each side's conclusion being the relative opposite or counterpart quadrant to that of the opponent. If opposing counsel appear to differ widely on their assessment of these quadrants – if this can be figured out or inferred from their communications – it is a potential sign of trouble. With competent counsel examining the same circumstances, there should not be much difference in their assessment of objective elements.

The clear-cut winner for a plaintiff is, by definition, going to fall into the "good-good" quadrant for the plaintiff and, by equal definition, the "bad/bad" quadrant for the defense. Absent some blunder, the "good-good" side is going to win, and wild swings from win to loss should not be a factor. Cases or claims that fall on the good side of the inside margins of the good/good quadrant might be categorized as "iffy," meaning iffy-good facts/good law." These marginal cases that are all on the good side might still be considered clear-cut winners where the iffy factor tends towards more to the good than the bad, or where a single factor on the good side is strong enough to carry the case over some lesser number of factors on the bad side, with the "bad" components thereby being more remote or unlikely.

An example might be an intersection case with a stop sign. The defendant ran the stop sign and collided with the plaintiff, and there are some injuries. Case starts out "good/good" (for the plaintiff). But investigation reveals that the plaintiff was speeding; under the law, a driver who is speeding may be held to have forfeited the right of way. We have to add a factor that is theoretically "bad/bad" to the mix. Bad facts = speeding, bad law = forfeits right of way. But it turns out that the "speeding" was just a slight variation over – 28 mph in a 25 mph zone, which is not a school or playground zone or other area of particular hazard. Driving patterns in the community indicate that most drivers run at speeds slightly in excess of posted speed; citations are not written unless the speed is more than 5 mph over the posted speed.

These factors might change the mix to "iffy/bad" – an iffy fact, against the bad law. On plaintiff's side, and keeping everything in perspective, the box goes "good/iffy." The task of the plaintiff is to put all the boxes together and come up with an amalgam rating for the case as a whole. She may decide to make it good/iffy – good overall, given only slight speed. Not surprisingly, in the overwhelming number of instances, the final result in most cases is going to be some version of "iffy/iffy."

The clear-cut winning case is not necessarily going to be easier to settle than one of the iffy varieties, for issues surrounding the extent of damage or amount of loss may lead to difficult evaluation problems. However, when all that is being fought over is how much, the process of evaluation and negotiation does not present the challenges posed by cases falling within the remaining quadrants.

The initial classification does not always hold throughout. Sometimes the case will start out looking like an admitted liability and move into the in-between category as more facts are uncovered and added to the picture. Sometimes it develops the other way. Here is an example of how a simple fact pattern can move from the "good-good" side to the "bad-bad" with just a few changes in the underlying details.

Plaintiff contends she tripped on a curb installed by the grocery store right at the exit doors from the store to the parking lot.

1. While other curbs in the center have been there for years, this curb was just put in recently. The walkway used to be a smooth ramp from store to parking lot. The construction barriers were up, but the warning signs were not there. The accident happened at night, the entry light was burned out and the entry was dark. The curb is 2" higher than the approved plans or construction standards allow, and the plaintiff is the fourth person to stumble and fall at the same place since the new curb was installed. She suffered a compound, comminuted fracture of her leg at the ankle, with many complications during recovery, which will probably leave her with some degree of permanent impairment.

2. Same facts, except: construction caution signs to "watch your step" were up, although there was no sign right at the curb. The specification called for the curb to be painted bright yellow, but this had not been done yet; a primer coat had been applied, making the curb an off white. The entry lighting was adequate and operating. Claimant was with her invalid mother, helping her down the ramp. She broke a small bone in her fibula, and was on crutches or in a boot for 3 months, but has fully recovered without complication.

3. Same facts as in number 1, except: the new curb is part of the redesign of parking and walkways throughout the shopping mall area just outside all of the entry and exit doors to all of the stores. It had been publicized for months prior to construction. It was approved by the city planning and zoning. The curb edge is painted bright yellow. The 2" overage was repaired in time, and the curb met all required standards by the time of the accident. The entry lamps had been repaired and the entry was well lit. There have been no previous complaints. Plaintiff was not wearing her glasses, which she needs to drive. She tripped but did not fall, and twisted her ankle.

From a plaintiff's standpoint, number 1 is a solid case. Good facts on liability and causation; good facts on owner's fault, and good facts on damages. The issue of "proper lookout" will be a jury issue, but the surprise factor, the poor lighting, the defective construction and the lack of warning weight heavily in plaintiff's favor. Matrix would be supported at good/good or certainly good/iffy-good.

In number 2, things start to sour. Still an unexpected curb in poor lighting, but better marked and with some warning signs about. The "proper lookout issue" becomes more troublesome for the plaintiff. Decent arguments both ways on liability. Still good on damages, albeit not as large. Sympathetic plaintiff assisting her invalid parent. Overall, a questioned outcome case by most standards; some might say it still leans towards the plaintiff, but clearly this case could go the other way. Maybe iffy-good/iffy.

In number 3, there is not much to like. Bad facts for liability, bad on the law, and bad on damages since simple sprain not worth much unless coupled with something else. From plaintiff's perspective, this is no better than iffy/iffy-bad, and perhaps this might even rate a "bad-bad" classification.

The point to take away here is small details can have considerable impact on the overall picture. Careful investigation here is essential. Thorough preparation and careful analysis is essential.

Suppose plaintiff in the second slip and fall scenario above rates his case as an in-betweener of "good facts/iffy law" with the good facts sufficient to carry the day over the bad law by odds in the range of 60/40 for the plaintiff. The defense may look at the same quadrant from the reverse, from the defense side of the matrix, and rate the case as being "iffy facts/good law" and conclude that the good law is sufficient to overcome the bad facts, by odds in the range of 60/40 for the defense. This difference in the quantum measurement of probabilities is what makes horses race. The parties are not flipping a coin here; the risk factors for one side are not the flip side of the coin flipped by the plaintiff, and it is common to find differences of opinion in the estimation of overall probabilities.

Category for the close case

When a close case or close claim is classified as a clear-cut winner when it should be considered no better than a strong in-betweener, this can lead to problems. Counsel invariably tends to overvalue the clear-cut winning case and the settlement dialogue may start off wrong. Counsel may misread the responses, and not listen to the nuances of the opposing offers. This may not be fatal to the overall effort, but it may make for some rough spots in the flow of negotiations.

On the other hand, classifying a case initially as strong in-betweener case where it might actually be a sure thing case does not lead to any serious problem, even if it later develops that there was a slight undervalue at the outset because of the miscall. This is because even when the parties are in general agreement on the liability issue, the defense values will always be lower than those of the claiming party. This means if the plaintiffs overvalues their side at the outset, they will be even further apart from the initial defense value, whereas a slight undervalue might encourage the parties to move together a bit sooner. There is also the aspect that counsel who categorizes the case as a questionable outcome will remain more sensitive to the element of risk, and therefore more intuitive and sensitive to the nuances of the opponent in settlement dialogue. The exchanges may be more responsive, and the negotiations may move more smoothly.

This means if an error is to be made, one should err on the side of uncertainty – treat the case as a strong but questionable outcome case until all levels of uncertainty are resolved.

The objective of this analysis is to establish some standards by which counsel can measure a case at the outset to make a determination of whether to accept it or not. The objective here is to take the acceptance of case out of the pure instinct or gut feel, and apply a rational basis to the decision. This will be refined further in the next chapter.

9
Winning cases refined

Most lawyers only want to deal with cases that are winners – either outright winners or in-between cases in which the winning probability sufficiently outweighs the odds of losing.

The clear-cut winner from the good/good quadrant is by far the easier of the litigated cases for the lawyer and the client to identify and evaluate. There is only one unknown variable at play, that being the dollar amount that might ultimately be awarded at a trial. Assessing value consists of estimating the amount that the court or jury would eventually award, and applying appropriate discounts for early resolution, savings of costs and fees, and finality. The negotiations for settlement may be more contractual than adversarial. These are not necessarily easy tasks, for even where the liability outcome may be obvious, the dispute over amounts due can be significant.

The next broad category consists of those cases where not only is there an issue over the amount of damage, but also where the underlying liability issue itself is in question. These are the cases where there is at least some question whether the defendant is liable for any amount at all. These cases are found in the mix of iffy/iffy cases from the table. The estimations are somewhere between a possibility and a probability that the plaintiff may lose on the issue of liability and therefore not be entitled to damages at all.

In this category of cases there are questions over liability, over the entitlement to damages, or both, and over the amount to be awarded if there is to be a verdict. They are referred here as the in-between cases, meaning "in-between" being a clear cut winner and a dead bang loser. The better of these cases will fall on the good side of most quadrants, with no worse than iffy or iffy-bad on the bottom. The mediocre here will have a sprinkling of iffy and iffy-good along with the good mix on top, and but still limited to nothing worse than iffy-bad on the bottom. The worst cases will be those falling in the iffy/iffy in half the quadrants and from iffy-bad to bad quadrants on the rest. These cases would probably be considered losers.

One would assume that counsel will be happy to accept the good/good cases and the in-between cases that are on the high end – all good or iffy-good on half, with nothing worse than an iffy-bad on the other half. In the in-between case, counsel must decide how far the balance must tip before it is too steep to take the case. Suppose counsel estimates that the better range of in-between cases will fall in the 60-40 range, with plaintiff winning 60%. If counsel routinely accepts 60% probability cases, under what circumstances will counsel consider accepting the case that is 50/50 on liability? How about 40-60? The final answer here turns on three elements: counsel's skill level, what the potential recovery might be and what the investment in costs is estimated to be.

Taking counsel's skill level first, if all the data that was used to refine the cases so far has come from national reports, specialty journals, discussion with other members of the bar, etc., it is probably safe to assume that the results are based on averages. A legitimate adjustment to an average is an adjustment for counsel's skill. This measurement can be absolute, meaning against the population of attorneys as a whole or relative, meaning relative to the opponent's skill level on this case. Supposing plaintiff's counsel is a seasoned, skilled trial lawyer with many successful jury trials. He might decide that his skill level, absolute against the population of lawyers, is worth a 10% adjustment to the average probability. He doesn't know who might be on the other side yet, so cannot make a relative estimate of skill. If the average probabilities might be 60/40, in his hands it would be 70/30. A case that is estimated at 50/50 normally would be 60/40 as adjusted for his skill level.

Where the cost of the process is minimal, and the potential recovery is large, counsel and parties can afford to take more risk to find out who wins and how much. Where the cost of the process goes up, the potential recovery requirement should be increased to make it worthwhile.

For example, suppose the case is 50/50 on liability, has a maximum potential for recovery of $25,000, and will cost $12,500 bring it to trial. Unless the client is very wealthy, is willing to pay the attorney fees, and insists on litigating "just because," this situation makes no sense at all at 50% probability. Consider: if the lawyer had 10 of these cases and tried them all, it would cost $125,000. (10 x $12,500). If he wins 50% of the cases, he would win $125,000 (5 x $25,000), meaning winning cases exactly on the button with percentages, and coming out exactly even on the money. The probable value of the case is $12,500 – being $25,000 x 50%. Lawsuits in this range are almost always vindictive get-even battles fought over matters of principle.

As long as everyone understands the reality of the economics, there is nothing wrong with this kind of action; lawsuits over matters of principle are exactly what courts are for; but if counsel and his client also intended the suit to be guided by sound economics, it is not. If counsel is looking to make a living at this, and his client expects to be made whole, the economics of the picture would have to improve considerably before it makes any sense to take the case.

For example, a lawyer very experienced and successful in plaintiff's medical malpractice cases, which are extremely technical and expensive to prepare and try, and which are almost always risky propositions, declines to take such cases on at all – regardless of the merits or probabilities – unless the potential damages reach something in the range of $400,000 or more. He says it is simply not worth the expenditure of time and money necessary to get one of these cases ready unless the potential payday makes it worthwhile.

Especially when taking these cases on a contingent fee, counsel must establish a set of threshold values to use as the decision point in accepting a case. Without threshold standards, counsel runs a huge risk of winding up with a shelf full of barking dogs, each demanding time and money without offering decent prospects of a profitable outcome.

It may be a young lawyer's dream to hang out a shingle and have multi-million dollar paraplegic case come through the door, but in the real world it would be just that – a dream. Big cases soak up lots of money, even where the fee itself may be on a contingency. Further, it is a recognized defense tactic to increase the impositional cost of the litigation, especially where it might appear that counsel and/or client are inexperienced and can be put under pressure with the enormity of what big litigation can impose upon an individual in terms of demands on time and money. The lawyer and client have to have the wherewithal to withstand these costs and stay current as they accrue.

No pending litigation?

Is it possible to negotiate a resolution to a litigable dispute without any intention of actually filing suit? The answer is a complicated "yes and no." Let's take the yes part first.

If both parties are motivated to settle, if settlement brings something extra to the table, and if the settling party knows that litigation is a potential action if settlement does not result, then maybe a mutual settlement is possible. The classic example are divorce settlements. In many cases, both parties are strongly motivated to settle rather than fight. Much of the negotiation will be integrative negotiation, rather than distributive, with both sides adding and reshaping the "pie" until the framework of a workable deal appears. The distributive negotiation will occur over specific parts – the value of a business being retained by one party, or the amount of spousal support to be paid and for how long. Settlement of these specific issues adds an immeasurable value to the overall resolution of the divorce, enabling progress to be made on many fronts. Peaceful negotiations to resolution with no threats or declared intent to litigate any issue may work just fine.

On the other hand, where the dispute is over a one-off event, with no lasting relationship to protect or respect, and no practical way of reshaping the pie or bringing additional values to the table, the "or else" of the existence of pending litigation is almost essential to achieve the maximum result from a negotiated solution. In order to get the other side to offer the maximum money available to get the case settled, there has to be something extra. Defendants will not generally cough up top dollars for settlements out of the goodness of their souls, or even just because they might theoretically owe the money. In most cases, they step up because they are already in the middle of the lawsuit, their money is pouring out every month to pay the defense lawyer, and they are opposed by a trial lawyer who has prepared his case and is ready to go. He is capable and competent, and has demonstrated with conviction, that if he doesn't get the case settled for what it's worth, he will take it into the courtroom and get it from a jury.

There are law firms who appear to take on personal injury claims with no intent of litigation. They put together a settlement package, not a trial package, and then set the case up for either a direct negotiation or mediation, where they settle for whatever is obtained with that effort. There was never an intent to litigate the case to the bitter end.

However, it does not take long for the defending insurance companies to figure out that these firms seek only negotiated solutions, without being prepared to actually litigate. As soon as this is realized, the maximum offers decline. These firms themselves do just fine on the volume of cases they handle with their share of whatever that can get. In some cases, however, the individual claims get settled for less than would have been available had there been the extra threat of a pending trial.

The wise lawyer knows that in order to convince an insurance company to take his position seriously, it is essential to actually prepare the case for trial. Even better might be if the lawyer actually tries a case or two to set the standard, at least for him. Best of all would be if he cleaned the insurance company's clock a time or two. Once the insurance companies know that counsel's guns are loaded and that he knows how to shoot, the settlement offers will begin to recognize the true value of the case.

Winning is relative

Let us take a closer look at winning. It is sounds like a simple concept, right? If plaintiff gets a verdict, the plaintiff is the winner. If not, he is a loser. It's a winner or loser, a light switch that is on or off. Right?

Not so fast. Supposing it is a case where if plaintiff wins, he gets some amount up to 100 chips, if he loses, he gets nothing. The chips can be of any value. To the casual onlooker, it might appear that any verdict for plaintiff, from 1 to 100 chips is a "win." Only the verdict for the defense, the zero, is a loss.

But suppose the client needed at least 90 chips to make it worthwhile, but the jury only awarded 10 or 20. To an onlooker who doesn't know any better, it looks like he still won, the case is still categorized as a winning case, and any mistakes made may be overlooked. But if the plaintiff really needed to get to 90 chips, and only obtained 10, isn't there a good argument that he still "lost" 80 chips?

What about the situation where if the plaintiff wins, he wins 100 chips, if he loses he has to pay the other side 50 chips. Now aren't the stakes of losing increased? If he wins, he only wins 100 chips. But if he loses, he not only loses the 100 chips he was hoping to win, but he also has to pay 50 chips to the other side – isn't the total loss here 150 chips? How solid does this kind of case have to be before proceeding is worthwhile? If the odds of winning were no better than a 50/50 chance here, are the risks worth it? Half the time he wins 100 chips, but the other half he not only doesn't win, he has to pay the other side 50 chips. Is this 50/50?

To bring this into reality, consider the common situation where the plaintiff's lawyer has the case on a contingent fee. If the case produces a verdict that does not return enough so that the lawyer's share taken as the lawyer's fee is sufficient to reasonably compensate the lawyer for the time and effort spent, isn't this a loser to the lawyer, no matter how much the verdict yields for the client?

Sometimes it's easy to label the basic winner and loser, but more difficult to value the result. Also, the value to the party of winning the case may be completely different when looking at it from the other side. Finally, the values needed can change as time passes and the situation of the plaintiff changes. In the contingent fee case, for example, the longer it takes to produce a settlement of a given value, the lower the relative value of that verdict will be to the lawyer doing the work. If it takes the lawyer a week to settle a case for 100 chips, his 1/3 fee is 33 chips, earned at the rate of 33 chips per week. If it takes him three weeks to settle the same case, his fee is still the full 33 chips, but it dropped to the rate of 11 chips per week.

As might be obvious, the assessment is easier and the plaintiff has greater control of the process, in those cases where the outcome is more certain – where the case is a clear winner, the defendant is going to be found liable, the plaintiff is going to get the verdict, and there is only one real question involved – how much will the verdict probably be?

The assessment is much more complicated, and the defending party may have much greater influence, where the case is an in-betweener of uncertain probabilities. The more doubtful the outcome, or the greater the element of risk that is involved, the more complicated the assessment of value becomes, and the more important are the value ranges that are created.

When it comes to settlement negotiations, each category requires a completely different set of mental gymnastics on the part of both lawyer and client in order to be prepared for the settlement effort. Assume the rule is that the firm is unwilling to proceed with any case where the potential verdict is less than X dollars unless the odds of winning are significantly better than 50/50; with the rule being the shorter the odds of winning, the greater must be the potential pot at the end.

But having all these positive factors in mind, there is still the chance of zero, and counsel must keep that possibility in the mix. Counsel must have a keen eye for all of the potential costs and probabilities in evaluating the case and a very sharp pencil to analyze the comparisons when what appear be offers start coming in. But in the last analysis, it is going to be counsel's intuition that will be the final arbiter on whether to take the case or not.

Counsel does need to establish at the limits for the type and size of case he is prepared to take on, whether individually or as a firm, in terms of the dollars available to invest, the potential expected recovery, and the risks or probabilities in terms of a percentage the firm is willing to take on. The limits should be both minimum standards – to not accept very small cases relative to the cost to prepare, or cases that are very expensive to present, relative to the probable verdict range – and maximum cases standards, being the most counsel is willing to advance in cost and the maximum size or complexity of case counsel is willing to undertake.

As counsel gathers experience, his personal boundary for acceptance can be shifted to allow more risk and greater cost, so long as counsel balances this with increased potential for recovery.

10
A roadmap through a negotiation

Whether the process occurs as a direct negotiation between the parties, or between the lawyers only, or is conducted with the assistance of a mediator, the steps to the process are exactly the same. A mediation is nothing more than guided negotiation. At the core of every mediation is a negotiation process, which will follow exactly the same path as a direct negotiation.

There are five parts to a negotiation, which we call: (1) the convening step, (2) the connection (3) the exploration, (4) the turn, and (5) the close. What follows is an overview and explanation of these five parts to show how they interrelate in the negotiation process, and how the steps may differ somewhat between a direct negotiation and a mediation.

The convening step

The step is nothing more than inviting the opposition to negotiation and, if the invitation is accepted, getting the first meeting off the ground.

A direct negotiation does not require much to this step, because by definition the parties to the negotiation are brought together by the very fact of the phone call to say, "Let's talk."

The *convening step* in a mediation is more formal. It consists of the administration required to agree upon a time and place, the process of selecting a mediator, and the process of getting everybody necessary to the mediation together for the meeting. It is usually handled by the lawyers, sometimes dictated by court order, and sometimes delegated to the mediator. However it is arranged, it sets up the process for the first real action involved in the negotiation.

The connection

The essence of this phase of a negotiation, whether in direct negotiation or mediation, is getting the individuals who are going to conduct the negotiation or participate in the mediation actually connected to the process, one by one. This is much more than mere physical presence, or the appearance of paying attention. This term is in the context of being "tuned in," or "committed." It does not have anything to do with any substantive issues. There is no need for anybody to agree upon anything substantive yet, but the thing will never get off the ground until all the participants are "connected."

The old saying, "You can lead a horse to water but you can't make her drink," can be applied to the negotiation process at this step. The parties can be ordered to negotiate, and are often ordered into mediation, but the order can't make them actually do anything once there. If the process is going to work, everyone participating must believe that it is worthwhile and want to make it work. The connection occurs when each participant actually reaches that mindset and "tunes in." It is difficult to define how to get one connected to the process, but it is easy to recognize when it has happened and it is unmistakable when it has not.

What is almost an absolute is that it has to occur or the process won't work. Nothing meaningful in a negotiation or mediation will occur until the connection step is complete. All participants necessary to the process have to be connected or the session will be a waste of time. There is no such thing as a "unilateral negotiation."

The room may be full of people, with everyone who was invited having shown up, but that does not mean anyone is connected to the process yet. Sometimes everybody arrives all fired up, and sometimes the first negotiation exchange is sufficient to wake everybody up and close the circuit. But usually it takes more than one exchange to get everyone plugged in. An exchange is the transmission of an offer and the reply; it is one completed loop of offer/demand and reply, and is the basic unit of action in any negotiation.

Where the parties starting valuations are far apart, and especially where the issues are complicated, the process of connection can be trying. A mediator can be of significant assistance here, to direct the process and translate what is required to move each individual towards connection.

When one side appears to stall efforts to get connected by making unrealistic demands or giving unrealistic responses, the opposing party may react in kind with random and equally meaningless replies, or it may choose to ignore the unreasonable demands and make what it calculates to be a bid that is a fair invitation to the connection.

The tactic chosen depends at least to some degree upon why the opponent is being unrealistic. There are three obvious reasons: (1) the lawyers are huffing and puffing for their clients before having to settle down, (2) it is the clients that are stuck, and the lawyers are allowing the clients to vent before insisting that they settle down, or (3) neither lawyer nor client is interested in the process, and without a change in attitude, the negotiation isn't going to work.

If the lawyers haven't settled down, responding with random replies just to mark time might be in order. One simply needs to be patient and wait for the opposing lawyers to come around. If it is the clients that are acting out, it may be wise to make a rational bid that shows the way to the correct path. If it is the last reason, that it isn't going to work, there is probably nothing anyone can do.

Perhaps a mediator can bring about an epiphany or force a gestalt to bring the parties around, which is likely to be the only hope under such a scenario. If it is in mediation, the mediator will probably let the mediation continue for three of four rounds while he unpacks various crowbars and wrenches from his bag of tricks, but if he can't get the bolts unstuck and a fire going, and there does not appear at least a glimmer of recognition of reality in the eyes of the recalcitrant party, an impasse will be called.

There are a myriad of reasons why a negotiation might fail at the gate. It could be a timing issue, the wrong individuals at the conference, a significant item of information that is missing or incomplete, or unresolved issues over the reach of the demands, to name only a few of the more common reasons. If the process cannot be started within a couple of beginning exchanges between the parties plus a shove or two from the mediator, it will probably have to be re-engineered to find and repair the linkage that is missing, and then restarted from scratch at a later date.

The point here is not to let the wheels spin needlessly. Negotiation is a voluntary process that requires all participants to be attentive. If they truly do not want or are not able to participate at this time, there is no way that they can be forced. If it's in mediation, the mediator should not give up until he has tested all the doors and windows, but if after a reasonable effort everything remains locked up, the mediator should call it a day.

Fortunately, as long as everyone has been paying attention up to this point, and as long as it does not appear that anyone feels forced or coerced into the process, failed negotiations at the gate are rare.

What usually happens is that as soon as somebody starts it, everybody will join and all will begin to climb off their high horses, put down their swords and shields, and discard their armor. Usually, too much has been invested in getting the parties to this stage of the case to allow it to bog down for too long in the unconnected phase. The lawyers do need to show their colors, and the client may need to vent. It may not all happen simultaneously, and one side may get a little ahead of the other, but these aims are usually accomplished within a round or two, and by then everyone is ready to settle down.

The exploration

The end of the beginning phase is not marked by a sharp edge or hard boundary. Rather, it comes from an awareness that real, identifiable progress is beginning to happen. The signals that the parties are connected come from the construction of the settlement dialogue, not from any external regalia.

Essentially, the offers or demands perceptibly shift and are no longer random. A foundation to the exchanges begins to become obvious, even though one may not agree with it yet. The numbers in the offers become messages, part of a dialogue, responsive to what has gone before and prescient of what is to come after. The dialogue is beginning to move in a clearly recognized direction, even though it may not be within any practical numbers yet. These are all signs that the connection is or has occurred. There is still no guarantee that the negotiation will get anywhere, but at least it is not likely to collapse for want of trying. Once both sides (or all sides in a multi-party conference) are indicating the connection, the process is ready to move onto the next step.

The heavy lifting in any negotiation is in the exploration stage where the parties get into the business of seeing if the ends can be brought together. This is the process of getting the parties from the mountaintops where they may have started on into a ballpark where a final answer might live. The objective here us not to find the right answer, or the exact number, but simply to define the area where the right answer might be found. There is no technical term for this location. The classic label was "trading range." The Harvard Negotiation Project refers to it as the "Zone of Potential Agreement," which is immediately shortened to the acronym ZOPA. The author, for all purposes and for over 40 years, has simply referred to it as "the ballpark," believing that everyone understands the concept of "an offer in the ballpark."

The objective the exploration phase of a negotiation is to get all the parties into the same ballpark at about the same time. Once the parties get into the same ballpark, they explore it to identify the various landmarks and features. If the process is going to work, eventually everyone will congregate in the vicinity of home plate. Not quite at the plate yet, for there are two important steps to go, but in the vicinity of the plate, and clearly in a position to be aware of the plate. This is when the objective of the exploration phase will have been realized, and the parties are ready to move to the next step.

Experience has shown that if all parties arrive at the ballpark at about the same time, the likelihood of success is increased. If a mediator in involved, it is the mediator's task to direct traffic and to make sure that one party does not get too far ahead or lag too far behind in the journey from wherever they started to here.

The negotiation dialogue has been likened to a dance, and although usually expressed with some degree of sarcasm, it is an apt metaphor. The pace of a negotiation comes from the structure of the dialogue; it cannot be pre-set or dialed in by the parties, nor can it be changed once started. When there is a mediator, it is the mediator's task to determine the beat and make sure that all parties attend to it. Whether it is a rapid-paced foxtrot or a stately waltz, it is essential that all parties correctly identify the beat and dance to the music being played. One cannot switch steps from a waltz to a syncopated cha-cha-cha in the middle of the song. It is not possible to "cut to the chase" unilaterally. The messages will get mixed up and misunderstood, and all that will happen will be confusion. A mediator can be of great value here.

As the dialogue matures, successful negotiators will be paying attention to the party's moves and responses not so much for the value of the move itself but for the value of the target or destination that the current move is pointing to, and they will be fine-tuning their own moves to the estimates that they are setting up as goals – the eventual expectancies and acceptances of value.

If the process is going to work, eventually, the ballpark will be identified and everyone will move themselves into it, all within range of each other and, in the best of cases, all within range of home plate.

On the other hand, if the process doesn't work, if all these assumptions appear to be in place but the parties still remain a great distance apart with movement stalled, then something is wrong. There is a core dispute of fact or law that cannot be bridged, there is a matter of principle at stake that cannot be compromised, there is a misunderstanding at play, or someone has their eyes tight shut. It might have appeared that a party was "connected" to the process, but really was not. Somebody is refusing to accept a material reality of the case or is insisting upon a capitulation when the facts do not justify such, or has simply decided not to play. Typically, the "eyes tight shut" syndrome is a plaintiff's malady, but it can strike either side. Unless rectified, any one of these maladies can be fatal to the settlement effort.

The point here is to recognize the situation as a problem in the process, repair it if possible, but not waste time trying to continue in the face of it.

Negotiation does not work all the time. When the process breaks down, stop. Identify and fix the process if possible, but if it is broken and cannot be restarted, then adjourn and get ready for trial. Having to litigate an issue is not necessarily a horrible thing. Everybody has a lawyer, after all, and trials are what lawyers do.

The turn

If the process is going to work, after an appropriate exploration of the ballpark, the negotiation dialogue will reconfigure as the parties literally turn the process toward home plate.

The tenor or feel of the negotiation will change. The structure of the exchanges will change. There will be a 'turning point" where the content of the negotiation messages change into a closing modality, just as an airplane turns into the landing pattern for landing. It is difficult to describe but cannot be missed when it occurs. This is next to the final stage of the negotiation.

If the parties can get this far, then unless somebody does something really stupid – which unfortunately happens more often than it should – the case is going to settle.

In practical negotiation, the claiming party will still be a little high, but not too high. The claiming party wants the paying party to empty their purse; they want everything that is in it down to the very last nickel and the lint that is clinging to it. To get this, the claiming party's moves are still bait, which has to be placed very close to and just above the paying party's nose, but not too high. The claiming party does not want the paying party to lose sight of the bait, even for an instant, but he wants there to be no chance of leaving any loot in the paying party's purse.

During the turn phase, the parties will make sure that all the parts of the deal are on the table. All important considerations should have been on the table by now. If any special or additional considerations need to be included, they must be up on the table during the turn. The last thing anyone wants is to move to the final stage, the close, and have someone then pull out a list of special conditions.

Additional requirements, such as confidentiality agreements, the exact time and method of payment of all money due, the manner in which the settlement will be documented – all these details will be brought out and decided upon during the turn phase. If all goes well, and there are no surprises, the parties will eventually, or very soon, be standing upon home plate.

The close

These are the final exchanges to seal the deal. The great danger here is that someone will decide that things have gone so well, that another round or two might improve the deal even more. One side may look down and decide that it is not home plate they are standing on, but a new ballpark to be explored. In the words of the famous Spencer Johnson, they decide to try to "move the cheese."

Parties can easily get caught up in the tempo of the negotiation, and not want to stop. This can be extremely dangerous to the process once into or beyond the turn, for if the process has worked up to this point, both sides may well be stretched to the limit of their willingness to participate, and it becomes essential if the deal is to be preserved that it close right then. If one side does not recognize the fragility of the deal, but insists pressing on – the taut bands may break, and the offended party may abandon the process completely and snap clear back to where they were at the beginning. If the process cannot be repaired, the settlement opportunity will be lost.

The second trap that can be sprung is for one side to suddenly bring up a list of special conditions to be met – snidely referred to as "oh, by the way's," as in, "Oh, by the way, we need the closing to be in Chicago next Tuesday," or "Oh, by the away, you will have to elect Harold's nephew to your board," etc. It is essential that all such lists be brought out earlier, certainly no later than the turn.

Experienced negotiators know enough to head off these kinds of calamities, and a mediator can be invaluable here. Barring some disaster, then, most negotiations close with the magic words, "OK, deal!" Or, "Close enough – split the difference and we are done."

11
The geography of a negotiation

At the beginning of a negotiation, the heavy lifting is not in finding the precise right answer to the problem. Rather, it is in identifying the area where a right answer might be found.

It does not matter whether this process is through direct negotiation or with the assistance of a mediator. There is no technical term for this area the negotiators are looking for, so throughout this book it has been referred to as "the ballpark." It is thought that everyone understands the concept of "an offer in the ballpark."

At the outset, the major task of a negotiator, acting directly or through a mediator, in a litigation negotiation is to get the parties into the ballpark for the case under consideration. This is accomplished by the means of constructing a negotiation dialogue that will move the parties from where ever they started into that ballpark. It is most helpful to a successful result if the dialogue is constructed such that everyone necessary to the solution arrives at the ballpark at about the same time.

Only when all of the parties are in the ballpark, and they have inspected the park and identified all the major landmarks, and when they are beginning to eye the area around home plate, that the negotiators change the tenor of the negotiation, and begin the dialogue intended to bring the parties to a final agreement.

The negotiation dialogue consists of a series of offers to pay or accept a given sum of money in order to resolve the disputes. The offers are passed back and forth, either directly or through a go-between mediator. Typically the claiming party starts high, and the responding party comes in low. The parties take strict turns, with each move after the opening being a response to the previous move. A party who has made an offer to either pay or receive a given sum does not make a new offer until there has been a response.

Occasionally, it happens that an offer will be made out of sequence, by a second move being advanced before there is a response to a first move. It is considered an error of process, as the party is said to be "bidding against himself." In the ordinary course, the dialogue, much like an auction, works to gradually move the numbers together until the numbers reach the ballpark.

In the early part of the dialogue, before anybody is actually in the ballpark, the numbers produced will not be acceptable to anybody. The early numbers are signals, meant to indicate to the other party where the ballpark might be found, how far out the parties are, and how big the moves need to be for both sides to arrive together. As the numbers converge, and the location of the ballpark becomes more obvious, the numbers being exchanged become more meaningful in defining where home plate might be found. It is only when both parties are in the ballpark and have identified home plate, and are actually approaching the plate, that the location of the final answer will begin to appear. As noted above, in the progress of the negotiation, this does not actually occur until the turn, the beginning of the final series of moves toward the close.

The early communications are often distressing to clients and onlookers who are not familiar with the process, when they hear an early offer from the opposing side that is either a huge overstatement or a fraction of what the expected objective might be. The significance of these early offers is not in the value stated but in the movement and rate of change from one offer or demand to the next. This movement signals the direction the parties expect the negotiation will go if they are ever to reach the ballpark.

The landmarks of value

In any case subject to a negotiated settlement there are three landmarks of value attached to the process for each of the participating sides in the negotiation. This will be the case whether the dispute is a simple claim or compound multiparty matrix, and whether the case is considered a clear-cut winner or an iffy in-betweener of questionable outcome. There is no magic or technical terminology here, either. Rather, these landmarks are just for handy reference, and are referred to as (1) the "aspirations," (2) the "expectation," and (3) the "acceptance."

In a clear liability case for a sum certain with no defenses – a promissory note case, for example – there may be no daylight between these landmarks, and no difference between the landmarks of the plaintiff and the defendant. But in the ordinary litigated case where there is at least some uncertainty or risk, there will be differences – the more risk and the more uncertainty involved in the case, the greater the differences within the three landmarks per side, and between the three landmarks of each of the parties to the dispute will be. There will seldom be a case where the claiming party agrees with the responding party on any of these values – nor is it necessary that there be any such agreement at the outset, or anywhere along the way until the very end.

In a successful negotiation, each party to the solution will move from the outer ranges of their individual landmarks towards the inner ranges in the task of first defining the ballpark, then moving to it, then exploring it to locate home plate, then moving to home plate, all the while making adjustments necessary so that eventually everybody is actually in the ballpark and standing around home plate. In the final parts of the dialogue, the parties will explore the differences in value between the final landmarks of the two sides, until a final number to complete the negotiation and seal the deal will become the obvious and acceptable last move.

The aspirations landmark. This is the home run for the party; it is the very best result that might possibly result if the case goes to trial and everything winds up on the favorable side. It is the outer boundary of the relevant negotiation dialogue for the bidding side. Although cases rarely settle for one's aspirations value, it is not unheard of. There are circumstance where capitulation to the party's aspirations may be feasible. Where the case against the opposing party contains relevant and horrible or revolting facts, the disadvantages of a public trial may be sufficiently compelling to cause the party to meet the claiming party's demand for the aspirations value of the case. Such capitulations are very rare and seldom require much in the way of negotiation.

In the normal case, the practical value of one's aspirations value is its utility in determining a starting place or an outer limit for the ensuing series of bids. It is a tool to use in the process of estimating where the ballpark is, how far the opposing sides are from the ballpark and where they have to go to get to the ballpark in good time. Whether the value is actually expressed or just suggested in the early bidding, everyone expects the negotiation to move from the aspirations values towards the vicinity of the ballpark. Sometimes, although not necessarily, the aspirations value will actually be used as a marker in starting the negotiation.

If the aspirations labels do not appear to fade rapidly as the negotiation dialogue continues, this is a signal of difficulty with the process. Responding parties need to exercise some degree of caution if there is not movement from the other side away from their apparent aspirations landmark. A re-evaluation may be in order, or further analysis, or some other preparatory step.

The point here is that if the case has risk, or uncertainty, and is otherwise an appropriate candidate for a negotiated solution, and if at least one party is unwilling to recognize this by moving off the aspirations value in the negotiation dialogue, the process is not working; the machinery is jammed and attention must be given to the process to finding the reason for the stoppage.

The expectation landmark. The "expectation" value is a more pragmatic estimate of the worth of the case to each party participating in settlement process, giving due consideration to all of the elements, good and bad, including the risks and probabilities and the uncertainties involved. The expectation value is the workhorse of the negotiation process, for although it is not necessarily the exact final value demanded for settlement, it is by definition what one party expects to be in the ballpark. The significant dialogue of the negotiation will be that which is created to move the participants on each side from the opening area of that party's aspirations towards the area of that party's expectations, in the anticipation that when both parties arrive the region of their respective expectations, they will find themselves in "the ballpark."

If the process is going to work, the parties will find that the expectation values of all the participating parties will land somewhere inside the ballpark, hopefully within striking distance of one another, and ideally within striking distance of home plate. In the author's experience, the closer the match is in skill level of the attorney negotiators, and the more equal and thorough their preparation has been, the greater the probability will be that the expectations values of all concerned will land in the same ballpark, and within a workable range of a final agreement.

Even if the initial expectation values appear to be some distance apart, if everyone has prepared adequately and there is a motivation to get the case settled, the parties will usually recognize the issues giving rise to the differences and make adjustments to their expectation values on the fly. The negotiation is not just exchanging numbers; the parties also exchange information about their claims and defenses, how they will respond to positions taken by the opponent, and their views on evidentiary considerations. The settlement exchanges, whether in a mediation setting or in direct negotiations, may be the first time that either party or their lawyers have heard the opponents' position presented by the opponents. It is normal as new information is learned to make supporting adjustments to these landmarks in order to continue to bring the ends together. It is not a sign of weakness where a party adjusts the expectation value or the final acceptance value – it is a consequence of constantly updating the analysis of the case and keeping the values current to the very latest information.

This does not mean that opposing parties will ever actually agree upon the expectations values of a given case. In fact, the assumption is that they will still never, ever agree upon this landmark of their case. This is plain human nature, is expected, and is perfectly okay. In over 50 years of negotiations and mediations by the author on both sides of the bench, the occurrence of an agreement by both sides upon the expectation value of the case only happened once. But even then, it turned out to be the result of a miscalculation by one side. In reality, as is established over and over: the claiming parties are always more optimistic about their prospects for success, and the party or parties on the defending sides are more pessimistic.

In the real world, and as long as the parties have their eyes wide open, it is probably sufficient to the ultimate process if the expectation landmarks wind up somewhere within the playing field of the ballpark, ideally but also not necessarily about equidistant from home plate. The expectation values are not etched in stone or forged in steel; they are estimates based upon estimates, and both sides are aware that adjustments may well be necessary to their expectations during the final steps in the negotiation process to keep these values relevant and in play. These adjustments are not the same as rolling out the acceptance value as the parties converge towards closure; these are minor course adjustments to the expectations landmark that can come at any time in the dialogue, as soon as anyone in control recognizes the necessity for such in the dynamics of the negotiation process.

The objective here is that when the parties do arrive in the vicinity of their expectation values, they will be in the ballpark and the distance between the values of the opposing sides will be reasonable – there will be a gap, but it will be a bridgeable gap, close enough to bring out the final values – the acceptance landmarks – being the values where the case can actually be expected to settle.

The acceptance landmark. The "acceptance" value will be a figure that is at or very close to the figure that will actually settle the case – it's the "expectation value" marked down on the discount or clearance table. It might well be the "drop dead" or "get-it-or-go-home" number, but in the more practical case it, too, will be a dynamic value, usually derived from the differences between the expectations of one party in relation all other parties involved in the negotiation. In the perfect model negotiation, when the parties arrive at their expectation values, they will find that their respective acceptance values exactly overlap the expectation value of their opponents – meaning that any number in the middle of the range of values between the expectation values of the parties will fall within all parties' range of acceptance.

The ideal case will look like this:

Claimant's side	Chips	Defendant's side
Aspirations	60	
Expectations	51	Acceptance
Acceptance	49	Expectations
	35	Aspirations

The expectations and aspirations of both sides completely overlap at 49 and 51, with 50 in the exact middle. Any number will be acceptable, with the classic solution being the midpoint.

In the ordinary case, the acceptance values of opposing parties will be close, and may even touch, but will often require additional concessions somewhere to bring about convergence.

Claimant's side	Chips	Defendant's side
Aspirations	60	
Expectations	52	
Acceptance	50	Acceptance
	48	Expectations
	35	Aspirations

The values touch, which should be sufficient. If they are even close, it should work. Where there is a gap between the acceptance values of the plaintiff and defendant, can the difference be bridged, or is an impasse inevitable? As usual, the answer is "it depends."

Claimant's side	Chips	Defendant's side
Aspirations	60	
Expectations	53	
Acceptance	51	
	49	Acceptance
	47	Expectations
	35	Aspiration

The gap here is two chips, which in practical case, should be bridgeable. One side or the other makes a slight adjustment to move into the other side's acceptance range, or the parties decide to split the difference.

It is not unusual to find that the plaintiff has been somewhat overaggressive in estimating its landmarks, or the defense side has been overly conservative, or both. If this is the cause of the gap, the parties should still be able to close, for the party or parties should realize that the landmarks are based on estimates only, and adjustments are not signs of weakness. On the other hand, if there is a structural difference behind the gap attributable to a substantive dispute, more work may be required.

In a mediation, an unbridgeable gap presents the probability of an impasse if a solution at mediation cannot be found. Whether the mediator will be able to assist the parties in working around a gap depends almost entirely upon the preparation given the case by the parties and counsel. The side that is better prepared is going to be able to identify the cause of the problem, recognize the solution, and work to communicate the need to the opponent. If both parties turn out to be equally prepared, the adjustments will balance and progress can be made. Where an impasse looms because of what appears to be an insurmountable structural difference in expectation values that neither side appears willing to bridge, this usually can be attributed to one of three circumstances:

First, and most common, is an irreconcilable difference on an essential fact that cannot be harmonized or compromised, and that affects a core issue of the case. Usually, fact differences can be accommodated in the risk analysis, and compromised. Rarely, but occasionally, a critical disagreement will exist upon a core fact central to liability upon which neither side is willing to budge. If compromise is not possible, a negotiated solution is not within reach. These are the cases that require adjudication for resolution – they have to go to trial.

Next is the situation where the effort is premature – not enough work has been done for the required analysis. The sides disagree on the fundamental category – one side insisting it is a clear winner, the other finding it to be an in-betweener with substantial risk, which is a disagreement that should not happen if everyone is paying attention and has done their basic homework. However, the views cannot be harmonized, and the difference in values will be substantial. This defect can sometimes be resolved by recessing the mediation to allow the side deficient in preparation a chance to catch up.

Sometimes differences in the skill level of the lawyers is so great that the lesser skilled counsel feel overwhelmed. They do not know what to do next, they feel unable or unwilling to move further, and they freeze. Impasse is inevitable. Fortunately, this does not happen often. Usually, the inadequately skilled will recognize their limitations and rectify the situation by associating or referring the case to skilled counsel well before the mediation.

If it is not recognized until the mediation, it will probably result in an impasse, for even if the lawyer does not finally recognize the problem, the client will, and will refuse to proceed further. The result in either case will be for the inadequate counsel to withdraw or associate in skilled assistance. The whole works can be restarted at a later time.

Finally is the situation where an element is missing. Sometimes it is the wrong person is attending the negotiation, sometimes a point of law or of fact on a core issue has been incorrectly developed, and needs to be tracked down. Either further research or a definitive ruling by the court or an essential deposition may be necessary. This element can usually be corrected by recessing and postponing the mediation or negotiation sessions until the missing element can be corrected.

The case settles when the parties realize that even though they may not actually reach each other's acceptance values, they are so close that further litigation is not worth the time and money it will take. One side, or the other, or both will make that slight adjustment required, and expressions like "let's split the difference," begin to emerge. They recognize that all of these values are estimates and approximations, and that slight or modest adjustments are perfectly normal. Unless a huge blunder is made, the negotiation is over – the case is settled.

Where all sides are connected and committed to the settlement effort, the aspiration landmark disappear very quickly in the earliest steps of the negotiation process. The acceptance landmark will only appear near the end, when the parties are very close.

This means that the expectation landmark carries most of the freight in the negotiation dialogue, with all of the strategies and tactical decisions from the early rounds up to the final moments being tied to identifying, measuring, developing, communicating about, and finally moving upon the expectation values of the parties.

12 Valuing the landmarks

Of the three values making up the landmarks of negotiations, two – the aspirations and expectation values – are figured out early. The third – the acceptance figure – may be roughed out in concept, but it will be finished during the negotiation, when the appropriate time arrives.

The workhorse of the negotiation dialogue is going to be the expectation landmark with the outer boundary being the aspirations landmark. There are two ways of getting at these two important parts of the process. Either work up the aspirations figure first and then adjust that value down to the expectation or calculate the expectation landmark first and then adjust it up to the aspiration.

The strong recommendation here is that the expectation landmark be derived first, with the aspirations value being a function of the expectation.

The risk of doing it the other way around lies in human nature, in that unless we work to keep reality in perspective, dreams can get ahead of reality. The risk, if one works up the aspiration value without the grounded anchor of an expectation figure, counsel will get too far out. Then, because the aspiration number us unrealistically high, the expectation will wind up too high as well. The safer way is to estimate the expectation value first, to keep the aspirations figure grounded in some degree of reality.

Determining the normal verdict

The first task in calculating the figures that will be used to plan a negotiation strategy is to estimate a standard or normal verdict for the case in question without adjustment for liability. The task is to estimate what a normal jury, under normal circumstances, would award on average for injuries or consequences of the breach in question without compromising or adjustment for risk or liability issues or any of the special adjustments attributable to the specific case in question.

The steps in this task are (1) separate the potential damages into the several categories that may be involved; (2) calculate a normal value for each of the categories; (3) combine the categories into a normalized total and (4) apply any general adjustments applicable to a total verdict. The resultant figure will then be used in the next step, to construct the landmark values necessary to the planned negotiation.

Damages available in litigation fall generally into four categories, depending upon the nature of the case and the certainty of the proof. A given case may include more than one category of damage. The combined amount of all damages within the given case is the predicted verdict. For the purpose of calculating normal potential verdicts, the four general categories are: (1) special damages in tort and specified contract damages that are fixed and undisputed; (2) special damages in tort or specified contract damages that are variable or disputed; (3) general damages in either contract or tort; and (4) punitive or exemplary damages.

The first category of special damages are special or specified damages deemed fixed and undisputed according to the certainty of the proof. In the tort action for personal injury, these damages will fall into the special damage category of economic loss for such items as past medical expenses, past lost earnings, the fixed cost of repair or replacement of property destroyed or damaged by the occurrence, and other items of damage, proximately caused by the occurrence in suit, for which an exact monetary value can be established by the proof. In a contract action, the fixed and undisputed contract damages will be such items as the amount due on a promissory note in a collection action; the balance of the unpaid contract where there is a fixed amount due, the benefit of the bargain if the amount received and the amount that should have been received can be proved precisely, etc. If the plaintiff recovers anything, he will be entitled to 100% of the undisputed special damages.

Special damages that cannot be proved precisely are either variable or disputed or both, depending on the proof. These are specific damages in tort or contract where the existence of some damage is certain if the cause of action is proved, but there is some question of the exact amount due. Examples include such items as the probability of future medical expenses or the value of lost earning capacity in the future in a personal injury action, dependent upon the proof of the actual likelihood of the damage occurring. In a continuing damage situation, the variable nature of the damages may be tied to probable length of time into the future he damages will continue to accrue. Depending upon the proof, this may extend to the probable life expectancy of the individual, which may introduce even another variable.

In a contract action, variable or disputed special damages may arise where the measure of damages is the estimated fair market value of property lost or damaged. Anytime the measure of damages starts out with the word "estimated" or "appraised," the damages will fall into this category of variable special damages. Variable special damages are not as uncertain as general damages, for there will be proof of specific amounts from which a range of values for the jury to choose from will be established – usually by expert testimony on future values, or differences of appraisers on current values – with no opportunity for a runaway.

General damages in both tort and contract are those which are proved to exist but which have no exact dollar value that can be calculated or assigned. General damages are characterized by the general damage in tort for pain and suffering alleged by a plaintiff in a personal injury action. General damage may be alleged in a contract action, where the breach is alleged to have caused a general damage to the claimant not specifically measured in calculated amounts. A breach that sullies the brand name of a business, or that creates a harmful stigma on the claimant's business interest may give rise to a claim for general damages. Here, there will be proof of the events giving rise the claim, but no specific proof of a dollar amount to place on the general damage component. The jury will be instructed that if they found the defendant liable, they are to determine the monetary value of the items of general damage based upon their own experiences.

Finally, punitive damages may be awarded in extreme cases, where the conduct of the offending party is outrageous, an extreme deviation from normal standards, and taken with a wanton and reckless disregard for the rights and safety of others. Punitive damages are not favored in the law, and generally are only available under special circumstances. In Idaho, for example, special leave of the court is required to even plead punitive damages, and if included, the punitive damage elements must be proved by clear and convincing evidence – a heightened standard of proof. Punitive damages are a tort theory and are not available in all states in contract action. They are available in contract actions in Idaho, as a tort theory of damage superimposed upon a contract cause of action. It might be referred to as a "con-tort" where the duty breached is measured in contract with the remedy measured in tort.

In settlement negotiation, punitive damages are seldom considered unless the case is truly outrageous, when such damages are virtually sure thing. In the normal case, the defendant parties will resist any allocation to punitive damages, but will instead recognize values for the normal categories of damage that are on the upper or higher range of damage rather than the expected normal or average. Thus, a case with a recognized risk of sustaining a punitive damage award will be valued by the defense as being in the upper range of verdicts for the normal damage categories but without any assignment of value for punitive damages themselves.

Here are some examples:

Example: a condemnation case is a type of case where the damages are measured under contract theories. A typical condemnation action may consist of a partial take, where the state takes of piece off the property owners land for the purpose of improving the adjacent highway. Only a portion of the land is taken, but the owner alleges severance damages in that the remainder is impacted by the take. In addition, there was some specific property damage left by the state in the construction project. The potential damages could be characterized:

- *Undisputed special damages*: Cost to replace a fence destroyed in construction; cost to repair and replace water line damaged during construction. The amounts are determined exactly by means of invoices for materials and labor and cancelled checks evidencing payment; the totals are not disputed. Provided the owner can prove the fence was damaged by the workmen on the state project, the jury should award 100% of the damage claimed under this category. The only verdicts available here are 0% if the damage was not cause by the workmen, or 100% if it was. Since here, the state is agreeing the damage was caused by the state, the normal verdict will include this element of damage at 100%, with the actual cost of the fence and repair being $15,540.
- *Variable special damages* consist of the fair market value of the property taken, determined by appraisal conducted by three appraiser, who testified at trial and whose appraisals are included as exhibits. The appraisals range from $50,000 to $140,000. The owner is entitled to some compensation for the taking of his land, which the judge will instruct is to be the fair market value of the property taken. Here, the condemning party will agree that the owners are entitled to some money, but may dispute how much. The jury verdict will be between $50,000 and $140,000. Since it will be undisputed that this property was taken by the state, and the owner is entitled to just compensation for the property taken, the verdict will have to be at least $50,000, and probably some figure in the range of $50,000 to $140,000.
- *General damage* consists of stigma damage the owners claim they are suffering in their enjoyment of the remainder of the property. They allege that the property remaining suffers from its proximity to the improved highway, and that the owners are losing money from the business operated on the remainder of the property. They are not able to prove with precision any specific amount loss. There is no actual interference with the property or the access to it, the damage is only from what the owner's

claim is the bad stigma, in that Native American burial ground was dug into and relocated. The owners want to claim $100,000 for the damage; the property experts think a value in the range of $10,000 more realistic.

Spreading these values onto a table would look like this:

Categories	Low Verdict	Mid Range	High Verdict
Undisputed Special	$15,540	$ 15,540	$ 15,540
Variable Special	$50,000	$ 95,000	$140,000
General – Stigma	$0	$ 12,500	$ 25,000
Totals	$65,540	$123,040	$170,540

With nothing else to go on, the claimant might choose the midrange total verdict as the normal verdict for use in the later calculations of the strategic negotiation landmarks. However, counsel may have special knowledge applicable to this type of case. For example, in condemnation cases, owner's counsel may contend that the juries almost always favor the landowner. Under these circumstances, the landowner may choose to adjust the normal verdict to a number midway between the midrange and the upper limits – which in the example might be a value around $151,790, properly rounded to $152,000 ($15,540+$117,500+ $18,750).

To work through the process with a typical case, suppose in a personal injury case the damages consist of the following:

- *Unreimbursed past medical and lost wages*, which can be proved to the penny and which are not disputed, in the amount of $54.678.90. Counsel would be forgiven in all circles if he rounded this value to $54,700, or even $55,000. The eventual total will be an estimate, and even though this value can be established to the penny, the slight difference introduced by the rounding to make the figure easier to use later will be insignificant.
- *Variable or disputed special damages*, outlined in an extensive life plan, to include future medicals, future home care, and future lost earning capacity extended out for the rest of plaintiff's life. The total is $1,156,000, which will be proved through expert witnesses at trial. The

defense challenges almost every element of the life care plan. The plan continues mental therapy for depression unabated throughout the claimant's life; the defendant contends that the need for mental health therapy will vary over the years, and may be eliminated entirely if the plaintiff learns how to compensate. The estimated lost earning capacity assumes a college education, which the claimant does not have, and extend throughout plaintiff's life. Defense maintains the plan significantly understates the actual earning ability of the defendant, and that much of his earning capacity can be restored with training to pre-injury levels within 5 years, and no adjustment for earning capacity is needed beyond then. Although defendant may never actually argue his numbers for damages to the jury, if all the defense objections are combined, the life care plan damages are reduced to approximately $342,000.

- *General damages* – the plaintiff is a paraplegic as a result of the accident, and if unrestricted general damages were available, they would be in the millions. However, the case is in Idaho which limits non-economic damages. The maximum cap is adjusted every year, and in 2016 was $342,030.36. Plaintiff maintains, and defendant agrees, that any verdict rendered will exceed the cap, and will therefore be reduced to the cap as required by law.

The table for tort damages would look like this:

Categories	Low Verdict	Mid Range	Upper Range
Undisputed Special	$ 55,000	$ 55,000	$ 55,000
Variable Special	$342,000	$ 749,000	$1,156,000
General - capped	$342,000	$ 342,000	$ 342,000
Totals	$739,000	$1,146,000	$1,553,000

With nothing else to go on, the mid-range for predicted normal verdicts would be $1,146,000. However, plaintiff is aware that most juries discount life care plans distrusting the economic projections and being overwhelmed by the enormity of it all. Plaintiff's counsel may take a middle value between the lower quadrant and the midrange for the values (keeping the undisputed specials at 100% and the general verdict at its cap). The adjusted normal verdict to carry into the calculations of negotiation landmarks, would be $942,000 ($55,000+$545,000+$342,000).

Expected values for uncapped general allocation

Constructing the normal verdict value where the elements of damage are fixed, or variable within stated range can be reasonably done by allocation across an estimated field from low to high based upon the proof of what the actual range of damages will be. For general damage amounts, however, considerably more research and effort is required.

The starting place for the construction of an the normal value for the general damage component of any verdict begins, as before, with determining what an average jury would award as a normal, middle range verdict, for the general damage element under examination, taking into account the negative aspects against damages but without consideration of any of the negative aspects of liability. It is the value of the damage case under examination as though the liability case was a clear-cut winner – one from the "good-good" box on the prediction scale on liability, but middle-of-the-road from the standpoint of money damages to be awarded. It is average verdict for the damages sustained in the case. In mathematical terms, it would be either the mean or the median of all hypothetical damage verdicts that might be discovered or imagined in the array.

The problem is that while there will be proof of the existence of damage, the witnesses will not be allowed to testify upon the dollar amount of such damage. The basis for this is that in general damages, the witness is in no better position to determine a value for the elements of general damage than the members of the jury. By definition, there will be no direct or actual evidence as to any specific value in dollars of the elements of general damage; the amount to set as damage is by definition a matter to be determined by the jury. The law says that juries do not need technical assistance in this area.

The task in estimating a predicted general damage component of any jury verdict for a hypothetical "good-good" damage case is to find or create a data set with sufficient size to present a reliable measure of the mean and the median values across the entire set. Since the end result here never rises to more than an estimate in the long run, it is not uncommon to find that counsel use a combination of sources, including estimates, in creating what amounts to a hypothetical data set for analysis. They gather as much information about actual jury verdicts as possible from whatever sources are available – and then fill in gaps and holes with their own estimates and estimates gathered from other sources to complete the work.

There are a number of jury verdict research services available on line which can provide insight into possible verdicts. Caution needs to be applied to their reports when applying the data to small jurisdictions like Idaho. The nationally published reports suffer from a lack of local data particular to the smaller jurisdictions. All of the services rely upon voluntary reporting or investigation. There is no service that purports to collect or report on all the verdicts. In smaller jurisdictions, the results are usually somewhat erratic. The actual trends in value of jury verdicts is peculiarly local, and a verdict trend in one area will have no relevance in measuring potential verdict in another. Trends in large, metropolitan areas will not be reflective of verdicts in rural areas or smaller urban regions. The research service may have a table of adjustments which they suggest be made to data extractions to localize the result to a particular jurisdiction, but these adjustments are purely hypothetical. The smaller area do not produce enough data from which reliable adjusting factors can be determined, either.

The problem is that the actual data sets collected from smaller jurisdictions, like Idaho, are usually too small to be considered statistically reliable either directly or in providing statistically reliable adjusting factors to correct the reported results from larger states or urban regions distant from the actual local of the study.

However, all this being said, the verdict research resources will supply an abundant collection of verdicts on almost any collection of injuries one can imagine.

It is more likely that counsel will rely upon empirical experience for most of the data to be used. The information can come from counsel's own experience, from that of other members of his or her firm, or from colleagues willing to share. Special interest groups within plaintiff and defense oriented organizations abound, some strong enough to publish regular journals, with most relying upon on-line blogs and chat groups. The caveat in seeking information from these areas is to try to obtain a full spectrum of results. It is not all that valuable in an objective assessment if the only information obtained from such sources are the grand slam home runs, unless the result is clearly labeled as such and placed up at the "outlier" end of the analysis chart.

Picturing a bell shaped curve may be helpful. If a number of verdicts from a number of typical "good-good" admitted liability cases of similar damage elements could be found, the distribution of verdicts demonstrated graphically should fit somewhat into such a curve. The average verdict of the entire array, or the mean value, would be precisely on the line representing the precise middle of the array, or the median.

In a perfect bell curve data set, the mean, median and mode are the same (The peak of the curve on the X axis of a perfect bell shape curve will reflect the average or mean of the data set; it also will represent the greatest number of values at that point, or the mode; and will finally represent the exact middle value of the data set, or median); in practice, these values skew. It will be difficult to ascertain a mode unless the date set is divided into ranges, and the mode simply refers to the range with the greatest number of values within. The more useful tools for analysis, then, when examining a sufficient set of unique verdicts, will usually be the mean (the average in dollars of all the verdicts in the array) or the median (the middle verdict in the array.)

If the data set is an evenly distributed bell, with few outliers, the verdict at the mean of all verdicts in the set is the common average verdict. Where there are outliers in the data set that appear extreme from the normal range of the populated data, the mean value might be skewed unreasonably towards the extreme outliers. In such cases, the median, or middle of verdicts in the set, may be a more accurate predictor of the most common verdict in the set. Or it may be appropriate to throw out the outliers – disregard the few verdicts that are extremely high or low.

For example, suppose counsel is attempting to value an uncomplicated but moderately severe injury case, and is assuming admitted liability for purposes of the verdict calculations. Through a variety of sources, counsel has developed a data set of equivalent verdicts in clear liability situations. Counsel identified 20 general verdicts meeting the criteria of typical facts similar injuries, and found from his examination that juries most frequently returned verdicts in the $100K to $150K range, generally clustering between $120K and $130K. The distribution is 17 verdicts between $100k and $150K, with 5 being between $120K and $130. One verdict came in above $200K and 2 were at or below $50K. In tabular form, his findings would look like this:

Verdict Range	Number
1. Under 50,000	2
2. 50,000 – 100,000	-
3. 100,000 – 110,000	1
4. 110,000 – 120,000	5
5. 120,000 – 130,000	7
6. 130,000 – 140,000	3
7. 140,000 – 150,000	1
8. 150,000 – 200,000	-
9 Over 200,000	1

If the data were to be set out graphically, the graph would approximate a bell curve:

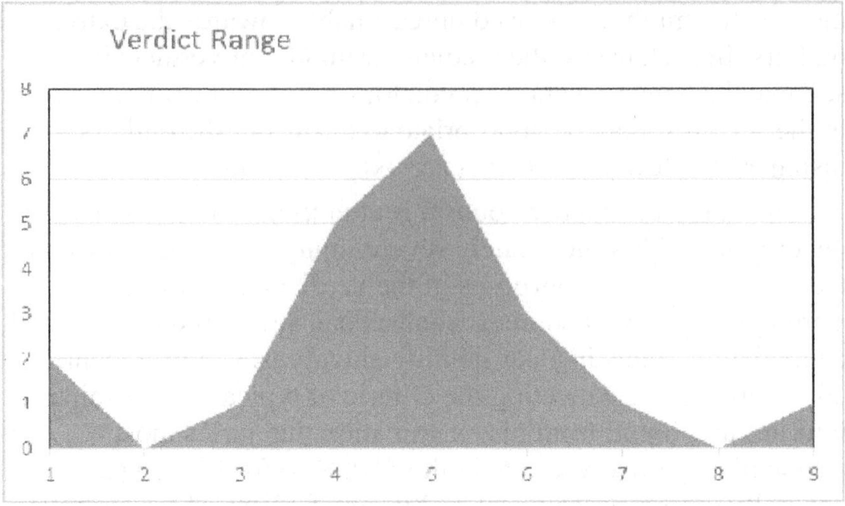

1. Averaging all 20 verdicts yields a mean, or average of $120.2K (rounded).

2. Counsel might decide to throw out the low verdicts under $50K and the one high verdict of over $200K as being outliers and not representative. This would leave 17 verdicts in the range from $100K to $150K centering on $125K at the median, or middle.

3. The numeric average of the 17 verdicts, based on the midpoint of each of the $10K ranges between $100K and $150K may be rounded to $123.8K, which one could round to $124K.

4. One might visualize this abridged data set appearing in a bell shape graph with the mid-point or median of the distribution around $125K and a mean or average of about $124K. A "good-good" hypothetical damage point estimate for the mid-range jury verdict value, then, might reasonably be an expectation value of $124.5K.

There is nothing precise about this analysis. The calculations do not have to be made with a slide rule, calculator or computer. Decimals are not needed; any result close to a barn door is close enough. It is rough calculation based upon vague data, and any eye-ball estimation will probably work just fine. Notice that editing the data set to omit the outliers did change the median/mean value slightly.

The missteps to avoid are starting out with too high (or low) a value from the data set being examined, and placing too much certainty on the value actually selected. To keep the total or final evaluation in balance, it is essential that the starting figures be somewhere within the predicted middle ranges of the expected values. It is also a misstep to treat these calculations as though chiseled in stone and not open to variation. Regardless of the size of the data set, or the source of the information, or the credentials of the publisher, these calculations are nothing but estimates upon guesstimates of the value of a future event.

Combining the results

The next step is to combine the results of the research for the general damage component of the verdict with the results of the estimate of the special damage element explained earlier. The result will be an expected total verdict by a normal jury under normal conditions.

Whatever the results are, the final step is to test the reported results against counsel's own experience, and against the experience of everyone counsel can get to listen. This is judgment and experience; how do the reported values calculated fit the actual case under consideration? Any adjustment here is a "seat of the pants" step that cannot be explained or defined but which is just as important to the process as the research. The adjustments include counsel's evaluation as to the overall fit of the figures derived from the research as well as specific adjustments that might be indicated on account of the exceptional factors, if any, that may be present in the case and which bear upon value.

Here are some examples of tweaks or adjustments from specific conditions that probably should be made, as appropriate (the list is not exhaustive; counsel may add any special consideration that applies):

- *The "wow" factor*. Certain types of cases may carry an aura that will impact the value of the case just from the nature of the injury, the nature of the accident, the stature of the tortfeasor, or a combination. The "wow" factor is hard to define, but easy to recognize. It is a factor or element of the case that can be expected to cause a jury to give an extra shudder or wince – to say, "Ooh!" or "Wow!" whether mentally or actually out loud – at the very mention or description of the circumstances. If the circumstances of the case under examination present any truly unusual or bizarre elements, consideration may be given to adjusting for a "wow" factor.

- *Inherent juror bias*. Depending upon the local culture, there may be certain aspects of the case that will turn a jury off – or on. In some areas, for example, bicyclists and motorcyclists are disfavored over automobile drivers. Physicians are favored in malpractice claims and may enjoy an initial advantage at trial, while lawyers are strongly disfavored by juries when they wind up as targets of litigation. In an employment dispute, the jury typically starts out on the employee's side. Individuals are favored over corporations. However, where two corporations are involved, the relative size is ignored – most juries completely overlook the concept of a "mom and pop" operation even where the other side is an industry giant.
- *Appearances may matter*. Depending on the location and community culture: tattoos, piercings and extreme hairstyles may have an impact. Clothing styles do matter, and extremes can be ruinous – particularly risky in a jury trial can be revealing women's clothing styles, sloppy or overly casual youth attire and anything that is dirty, wrinkled or worn through. Ordinarily, these elements can be cured by counseling the client towards appropriate appearance at trial, but if the client is not going to take the lawyer's advice here, or if there is going to be photographic or video evidence at trial of the client in compromising situations, some adjustment to value may have to be made to avoid a sting.
- *Alternative medicine*. Sometimes resorting to alternative medicine can work well – as in when the client goes searching desperately for a cure that traditional medicine cannot help. Sometimes it will flop -- as in when the client

goes searching desperately for a cure that traditional medicine cannot help. Unfortunately, it may not be known that the alternative medicine is going to be viewed with suspicion until it is too late. Many juries do not trust chiropractors. Acupuncture, or any esoteric Middle Eastern or Oriental treatment may be suspect in a rural community, yet be perfectly acceptable in a more urban venue. Medical marijuana is an explosive subject everywhere that is just beginning to rear its head.

- *Criminal records or unsavory pasts*. This is always a puzzle when the client has an unsavory past – whether to bring it all out or try to bottle it up with *in limine* rulings. If any of it is going to come out, the better plan may be to get ahead of the issue and bring it all out. If it is coming out, counsel must take into consideration what the jury is likely to do with the information in considering their verdict.

These adjustments may not need to be made, and they certainly do not always apply. It is a judgment call whether and how much they might affect a verdict. Counsel may well be aware of other factors which may bear on the value of the case or the probabilities of any outcome, and should freely add to the listings here.

What must be emphasized is that all of this work is just preliminary. The values are estimates, and are subject to adjustment right up to the last gasp in the actual negotiation, whether direct or through a mediator, and whether it is deal or no deal. The real test of how these preliminary landmarks and estimates of value will work will come then counsel finally shows this stuff a mediation or negotiation and tries to get the opposition to agree.

With an estimated mean or middle value in hand, adjusted to counsel's satisfaction, the expectation value is in hand, and the task is almost done. The next task is to take this value and adjust it to the aspirations value, thereby setting up the two essential landmarks necessary to begin a negotiation.

Aspirations value

It makes sense to construct the "aspirations" value after completing the preliminary work on the "expectations" value, because the expectations value is the more important of the two values, and because counsel and client are not likely to lose sight of reality in when trying to come up with a realistic aspirations landmark if this comes after establishing the expectation landmark. If counsel does it the other way around, and works out an aspirations value first, and it turns out to be too high, he may find it much harder to adjust his sights and the sights of his client down to a realistic expectations value.

While the "aspiration" value can be a pure pipe dream, it will be more useful in the negotiation process if it can be an actual declaration of what somebody – usually the claiming party's lawyer but sometimes the claiming party themselves – figure might actually be achieved in a jury trial if everything goes right. One lawyer once defined this value as, "one dollar less than the amount that the judge would take away from the plaintiff if the jury returned such in a verdict." Obvious places to look for the "aspirations" value is the top derived value for the case as reported anywhere in the specialty reports that is not, itself, an obvious outlier. This might be the verdict on the high end of the bell curve of predicted verdicts that lies within the curve, or the top dollar verdicts recently reported in topical journals and newsletters of trial organizations that have been sustained on appeal.

Even though the "aspirations" value may not actually be used in the final settlement result, it is an important part of the process. It is a potential result if the settlement process breaks down and the case actually goes to trial. If accepted as a viable number and not pure pie-in-the-sky, it is part of the risk factor for the opposition to bear in mind.

The process of settlement begins with the very first exchange and if it later turns out that the figures used in the first exchange were not just a made up but were actually connected to the case, and that there was some thought demonstrated in selecting the number – counsel will have added something to the element of trust and credibility. The value will lurk, and while it may not be much it will be something. That is enough to make it worthwhile to construct the "aspirations" from factors actually belonging to the case rather than pure wishful thinking.

Acceptance value

This is the get-to-here-or-go-home number. While a party needs to have a rough idea of an absolute number that cannot be breached in mind from the very outset of the negotiation, it is a sound idea for this value to be dynamic – to have some flexibility to adjustment as or if new information is learned at the conference that indicates modification is needed. When the parties are all in the ballpark and can see each other's figures, they can determine for themselves what it might take to bridge the gap.

When both sides actually reach their expectation values in a negotiation, even though they are examining exactly the same set of facts and law, they will invariably still remain some distance apart.

Also, the greater the risk, the greater the distance there will be between a well thought out expectations value and the acceptance value attached to it. Finally, the more unusual features from the list of discretionary adjustments there are in the mix, the greater the distance between expectations and acceptance. To say it another way, the more risk in the outcome and the more unusual features the case presents, the less predictable the final outcome will be and the greater the necessity to keep some room for flexibility before slamming the door on the deal.

When the parties reach the limits of their expectations values, and they are still some distance apart, both sides will usually have a sense whether the gap can be bridged or not. If both sides believe the gap can be bridged, the negotiation dialogue may well continue without even a hiccup. But if one side is willing to keep negotiating while the other side is showing some signs of resistance, both parties must pay attention. The read maybe that one side is closer to their acceptance value than the other – and there is not as much maneuvering room left as it may appear. Someone may have to adjust if the deal is going to close.

When a gap is closed between the acceptance values, it is a recognition of the classical rule in bargaining that the final value will invariably be the midpoint between the last two rational offers. In the perfect world, the acceptance values will just touch – the edge of each party's acceptance will touch the edge of the other party's acceptance. Some gap is more common, meaning the task for each side is to explore the gap until they identify more precisely where these values touch or overlap, or come the closest. Then they fashion a bid or series of bids to get there.

In the more mundane arena where many lawsuits live, and where any distance within a barn door's width is close enough, there may still be a gap, and one side or the other – or both – will need to make a bigger adjustment to finally settle the case. This will only happen where both sides are very close and both counsel determine that it makes no sense to continue the litigation. In the classical case, offers to "split the difference" make their appearance. This is why the acceptance value must have some degree of flexibility.

The acceptance value serves as a safety valve. Negotiation is a tool with many facets. The straight give-and-take of the dialogue, with the positions gradually converging, is at the heart of the process. In addition to the information and the analysis of the case – the strengths and weaknesses of the positions – there are other influences of significance.

The three major influences in addition to the substantive issues in the case are time, power, and pressure. More will be said of these influences later, but for now the point to be made is that the determination of an "acceptance" value at the outset is a safety valve to prevent the shifting dynamics of a negotiation from overwhelming a party because of these external influences. It is one thing to make an adjustment from one's expectations value based upon new information gathered at the negotiation that actually bear upon the strength or weakness of a position. This give and take is the essence of bargaining.

But where a potential cave-in might be the result of unequal power, or of pressures from external sources, or because of the simple element of time, then a rationally based acceptance value as the absolute minimum can be a safety valve – not to be released unless and until counsel and all parties affected are satisfied that any final adjustment to the acceptance value is a necessary adjustment that will directly facilitate a settlement and is based upon the welcomed developments of the negotiation, and is not a forced unilateral response to the influences of time, outside pressure or power. If counsel and the parties are willing to accept the final result despite these influences, they are doing so with eyes wide open. In a hefty multi-thousand-dollar case, letting the other side have the last word for a measly $500 adjustment to the announced best, last and final may be a blatant concession to time, pressure or power, but it also could be a perfectly rational concession as long as it gets it done today – right now – and once and for all.

The acceptance value should be of much firmer stuff than the expectation value, but it still should not be set in concrete all the way down to its last dollar. The expectation is clearly an estimate and is intended to be adjustable when reason and necessity dictate. The acceptance value should be intended as the bottom line, as a value not to be exceeded – unless an adjustment is absolutely necessary to get the thing done. There must be a little room for wiggle to prevent the making of a dumb decision over peanuts.

One last aspect of the acceptance value may arise in the case of the little guy against the insurance company. Usually, the company has a strong business motive to get the case settled, if they can do so within the value that has been established within the company for the case under examination. Assuming competent counsel for the claiming party and adequate preparation, the company will have a "not to exceed price" that it is prepared to pay before it lets the case go on to trial. It would, of course, prefer to pay less, and will strive to convince the receiving party to accept less.

The claiming party's objective should be to find out what the true top dollar is. The claiming party should not close down a negotiation for any reason until the company has revealed all the money it has. This means that the acceptance number of the claimant is an index but not a barrier. If the company is nowhere close to the index, and counsel can see no hope of even getting close, claimant's counsel may suggest that it is a waste of time without even looking further. But if the company gets within range, then the rule should be that the bidding does not stop until the company calls it off, not the claiming party. This may require that the claiming party allows the border of its acceptance value to creep a little before the company rolls out its final offer.

When this offer is rolled out, the difference between it and the hoped for acceptance value may be a significant amount, but it will be a difference that is within a number the company believes the claiming party cannot afford to litigate over. Not infrequently, the offer proposed as last, best and final will be accompanied by advice that this is as high as the company can go; if it is to go any higher, it will require approval from a home office valuation committee; and that committee will not meet again for two more weeks. So, take it or leave it. This is a frequent version of application of the influence of time and power.

The problem is that the company is usually right. They have picked a number that is right outside claiming counsel's comfort zone. This is where the steel parts of the acceptance value come into play. Are they bluffing? Can the claiming party afford to test them? How big a deal would it be to wait another week or so to have the home office committee take a look at this thing?

The existence of the carefully considered acceptance value allows counsel to make this decision from a basis of sound strategy and tactics, and prevents counsel and client from being steamrolled by pure pressure. There is nothing wrong with accepting the company's money. But the acceptance value is there as a check; it was objectively arrived before any real pressure was applied to serve as a tool in just this type of situation.

While counsel may certainly decide to waive the barrier and accept the money now, having the acceptance value in place as a landmark provides the machinery to decline the defense LBF – last, best and final – offer and head for the elevator with an actual plan in mind, knowing that deliberate consideration has been given to the issue.

Time–value of money

For cases that will be tried within a few months, the time value of money factor may not apply – the process to determine it is too finicky for the small amount returned. But where the settlement comes early in the case, with a trial perhaps as much as year or more off, or if counsel believes an appeal might intervene before any judgment rendered would be fully collectible, an adjustment for the time-value of money might be useful. It has not been included in the general discussion, because it is viewed as being too far into the weeds for most situations.

The theory behind the adjustment is that money paid now to satisfy an obligation that will not actually be due until some future date (i.e. a settlement amount paid now to satisfy a potential judgment which won't come into existence until some future date) can be discounted. The discounted rate is determined by calculating how much money should be paid today which, if invested at a reasonable rate of interest, would grow to equal the sum to be due when the future event occurs.

To illustrate: Suppose a party is entitled to receive $100 one year from now. How much would be required now which, when invested at a reasonable interest, say 3% in a CD today and due in one year? The answer is approximately $97, for this amount invested at 3% interest will yield approximately $100 in one year. [The exact amount is $97.09, being the product of the formula $PV = FV/(1+i)^n$, which can be applied to any amount, at any rate of interest, and deferred for any length of time. In the real world, this is what computers are for or why they put the financial keys on a business calculator.]

This adjustment is a bit sticky for any of the negotiation landmarks in general – since these overall values are all approximations, subjecting them to an adjustment based upon a formula calling for accuracy to a second decimal place asks too much. The only justification for bringing it out on the acceptance landmark is where that mark is deemed to be the barrier – the drop dead number that neither counsel nor client will budge from. If such be the case, then a finicky formula with a precise answer may be the solution to crack through to an adjustment.

If after thoroughly negotiating the values, the parties find themselves at an unbridgeable gap that cannot be closed without some rational basis other than "just because," this factor may serve that purpose. The receiving party can subtract from its otherwise bottom-dollar acceptance an additional amount to reflect the discounted rate of the money it would receive.

Conclusion

In the final analysis, the very last tweak to apply will always be the lawyer's "feel" for the case.

If after evaluating it all, it feels like the numbers are all too much, counsel can scale them back; if counsel is satisfied that there is more value to the case than is reflected in the calculations, the target numbers can be adjusted forward. The lawyers are going to have to use the final valuation figures and work with them in any negotiation, so the numbers have to be values in which they have confidence.

The more experience counsel has, the more times they work through these exercises, the easier it will become to arrive at a comfortable value to carry into the negotiation.

13
Adjusting for risk

The values being calculated up to now have been for undiluted damages where liability was not an issue. The figures can be used as the basis for negotiation in any undisputed liability case where the claimant is going to win, and the only issue is how much.

Next must come the circumstances where the first premise is not accurate; it is not an undisputed liability case. Where there some predictable possibility that the claimant might lose and take nothing, can this type of case be accurately valued for settlement purposes?

The answer is, of course.

Talk to the handicappers and actuaries in Las Vegas, Reno or State Farm Insurance. Calculating the odds on the outcome of a risky lawsuit is no different than calculating the house odds, say, on a roulette wheel or craps table. It's a little more iffy maybe, because the lawsuit does not include the certainty of two six sided dice, or a 38 slot wheel with 2 slots reserved for the house. But the principles of figuring the odds and probable payouts are exactly the same.

Adjusting for risk and probabilities

Many of the cases involved in extensive settlement efforts will be properly categorized as iffy in-betweeners – cases drawn from one of the "good/bad" or "bad/good" quadrants, or anything with a measure of "iffyness." If there is any significant risk that the case may be lost in the entirety, it's necessary to factor that risk into the construction of the values to be used in any settlement negotiation.

The landmarks for value as calculated to this point are only starting numbers where there is risk involved. They assume a risk-free trial, with only the actual amount of the verdict in play. Where there is risk involved, which will be in all of the instances we will be dealing with from here on out, the next step is to place these landmark values in some relative position with respect to the actual adverse aspects of the case being examined.

There are two general classifications of adverse results. The simplest case is where the adverse result is a simple loss – a zero. The more complicated cases are where there is a counterclaim, and where the adverse result can be a negative verdict of some proportion in favor of the opponent.

Whether the risk being assessed is a simple loss or a complex set of possible adverse verdicts, the process is essentially the same. Establish a value of each of the possible verdicts in the case as though each were an isolated "good-good" admitted liability case; determine the probability of each of the possible verdicts as against all other verdicts; and then combine these values to establish a hypothetical handicapped value of the whole.

Taking up the simple loss case first, the explanation here is that it is a good case, but there is a chance that it might be lost – the jury may disagree with a core fact issue, or the judge may instruct on a legal issue differently that claimant's counsel hopes, leading to a defense verdict. Everyone generally agrees that most of the time the plaintiff will win, but some of the time the plaintiff will lose.

The quantification of the probability of winning is purely hypothetical. There is only one case, and it can only be tried one time. There is no way to actually verify the validity of the odds determined.

There is no way that this single case can ever be both a 60% winner and a 40% loser at the same time. There is no opportunity to test try the case 10 times, or 100 times or whatever statistical number would be required to establish to certainty what the odds of the next trial should be. The subjective variables of a trial cannot be defined with the precision of a six sided die or a 38 slot wheel, so we cannot define a mathematical model to test all the variables to a precise mathematical answer, as can be done with a crap table or roulette wheel.

The answer is empirical knowledge. Experience. The collective opinions of lawyers who have been there. Or, in practice, all three. Losing is always a sad day for the losing party and counsel, of course, but losing the in-betweener case is going to happen some of the time – it is an inherent probability of the case that no amount of preparation will change. One veteran of the law once said he figured if he was winning every case he brought to trial, he wasn't trying enough of them.

In the simple analysis, when the case turns out to be a winner, it can be expected to bring in verdicts in the range of the "good-good" clear-cut winner value, and when it turns out to be a loser, it returns a zero. The jury will never return an in-betweener verdict based upon the probability of winning. But that does not mean that a value for the in-betweener case cannot be found.

In the modern age, few parties can afford to take the chance of a loss. Unless the litigation is truly over a matter of principle, or is setting a precedent for future cases, or fits some other circumstance where an adjudicated result is essential, most parties are willing to seek a compromise that eliminates the risk. They give up their chance for full and complete compensation in exchange for a lesser amount that recognizes the risk and eliminates the chance of zero.

Before trial, the pure economic value of the case as a whole is the simple probability value of winning the case times the probably verdict if the jury decides in plaintiff's favor.

This can be probability times the expectation landmark just constructed, or the aspirations value adjusted, or the acceptance value adjusted. Or the starting value can be any value that counsel wants to use. The closer the value is to a valid prediction of the future winning verdict, the more accurate the rest of the calculations will be.

The process can be stated as a formula:

$$S = (V \times R) - C$$

where S is the value of settlement; V is the probable value of a winning verdict; R is the Risk, or the probability of winning the verdict stated as a percentage decimal value; and C is the total of the unrecoverable litigation costs which will be avoided if the case settles now.

If the case is more complicated, and includes potential negative verdicts for the opposition – a third and possibly fourth adverse result will occur some of the time. In such a case, the possible verdicts are: (1) plaintiff wins, defendant loses; (2) plaintiff loses, defendant wins; (3) both sides win – the verdict becomes a net offset amount of the two claims; and (4) both sides lose. The task of evaluating the case for settlement is to determine the realistic probabilities of each of the possible outcomes, and factor those probabilities into a single value which would apply to the case as a whole. Exactly the same process is followed for the multi-theory, multi-party cases – it just gets more complicated in the arithmetic involved.

The steps in the calculation are: first, to break the case into as many discrete pieces as there are potential verdicts; second, to determine a hypothetical "good-good" trial result for each of the pieces; third, to determine the probability of winning each possible result in terms of a percentage; fourth, to estimate the overall costs to be saved if the case is settled now; and fifth, to then combine the values into a single value of the whole. Care must be taken that counsel uses the "expectation" value of the hypothetical "good-good" piece under examination and not the "aspiration" value.

Determining the risk factor or probability

In days gone by, it was not uncommon for an old time litigator to say, "If we try this case ten times, we will win it seven times and lose three" Where stated as a fair estimation of potential outcome and not a pure bluff, this sort of determination was purely based on experience. In more modern times, some insurance companies have actually set up computer programs to accomplish the same thing. The insurers that use the computer program to assess risk are very large companies, with huge list of claims pending. From the observations by the author, it is difficult to determine whether the computer is actually assessing the risks accurately, or the companies are using the computer number to force the results they want. The estimates from those with experience may be just as accurate.

To convert these clichés to a probability percentage, divide the number of estimated wins by the total cases in the data set. The probability of winning the crusty old litigator's case is 70% – seven wins divided by ten trials. The probability of losing is 30% – three losses divided by ten trials. There is nothing more involved in these calculations but fifth grade arithmetic at worst, certainly no more complicated than junior high stuff.

The result is a guess, of course, but an educated guess based upon the lawyer's or claims manager's practical observation over the years. Moreover, it will prove more than enough to guide that lawyer or claims representative in any negotiation over the case.

This basic estimate on the probability of winning needs to be made on every case where a negotiation to value is expected, and where the entitlement to the verdict or outcome could be in dispute, whether the negotiation is going to be direct or by mediation, just as soon as the expectation landmark is established. If the "good-good" hypothetical expectation of a clear-cut win without further consideration or adjustment, is $125,000, and the unrecoverable costs of going forward with the case from this point forward might be $10,000, the settlement value of the case if it were an actual in-betweener with a 70% probability of winning, would be in the range of $77,500. ($125,000 x 70% - $10,000) Note, this is not the value to maximize recovery on a good day; it is the value to reduce the risk of loss on a bad day.

The problem is not the arithmetic; the problem is developing reliable data upon which to perform the calculations. Everything is going to be in estimates. Sometimes, the estimates can be backed up with research, but more often not. An insurance company or large corporation with substantial exposure to cases of the sort under examination may have statistics of wins and losses from actual cases similar to the instant case available. Some insurance companies have computer programs to assist in making these estimates. But no matter how fancy the trappings, at the bottom of the best of it will be the estimates of some crusty old trial lawyers with experience, working hard to make their guesses look more precise.

Sometimes they are willing to share their data, and sometimes not. Where the opponent is an entity with skill and resources in this area and does not share its actual data, counsel should be cautious in the face of intractable positions, and be alert to the adversary's reasoning. It may be that the adversary has more specific and measurable information about the case than mere guesswork. Sometimes, alert counsel can glean an answer that is close enough from the communications, whether the adversary intended to share or not.

Sometimes the estimates can be backed up with research. The same jury verdict outfits that publish national reports on liability factors can be useful here. The locality of verdicts makes national jury reports difficult to use to determine or predict the amount of any verdict in a given locale. But the applicability of facts and law to who wins is not subject to the same local vagaries. Using a national report that is thorough in reporting all results – adverse results as well as big wins – can be useful in predicting the probability of a win or loss, no matter what the location.

Using mock juries or focus groups is a method being used in cases large enough to warrant the cost. These devices are not cheap to set up but the results can be illuminating. One prominent lawyer explained that he always used a mock jury in the larger cases – not so much for help in predicting the amount of potential verdicts, but for what could be learned from the discussion among the mock jurors about the liability features of the case – which is at the heart of the probability determinations.

The upshot here is that the best resource for determining the probability of winning or losing is the lawyer's experience. The time-worn method of comparing the case under examination with other cases tried by the lawyer and within his firm, and with stories provided by colleagues of their experiences, and using this compilation of personal empirical data as the resource to estimate the probabilities.

If there is no other effective way to estimate the impact of the negative aspects of the case, consider it to be a coin-flip and call it 50/50. The objective is to establish a very broad estimate of the odds on winning or losing the case in a situation where there is chance that the opposition can win. Whether the true odds are 60/40 or even 70/30, as long as one keeps in mind that it is only a broad estimate, using 50/50 in the settlement estimations should prove to be close enough for purposes of finding the ballpark in negotiation.

If counsel cannot bring themselves to rate their own case as no better than 50/50, then counsel is certainly free to make it 55/45 or even 60/40. These are estimates only – all of this stuff is educated guesswork, and it is essential that counsel not get locked in to believing in the precision of any of it.

Workbook examples

Here are some example of how a case could be worked through all of the analyses steps to arrive at the adjustments for risk, and then applied arrive at the adjusted values for expectations and acceptance for both a plaintiff and defendant.

1. *A slip and fall case in grocery store.*

Plaintiff slipped on some ice cream that had been spilled by another customer. Spill remained on the floor for at least 25 minutes before the plaintiff came upon it and fell. She severely twisted her knee, tearing ligaments and damaging the joint. Many complications later, the knee had to be replaced. Plaintiff's values before consideration of risk: Aspirations, $500,000; expectations, $425,000; acceptance $400,000. Estimate of unrecoverable costs, $5,000.

Typical liability problems with slip and fall; ice cream spill was visible on the floor if the plaintiff had been watching where she was going. Probability of winning, 60%. No counterclaims. Defense generally agreed with plaintiff's assessment and values before consideration of risk, but defense put the risk at 50 – 50. From the defense side, the unrecoverable costs are negligible and are not considered.

Plaintiff's side:	Defendant's side:
S = (V x R) – C S = ($400,000 x 60%) – C S = $240,000 - $5,000 S = $235,000 New expectation: $235,000 New acceptance: $225,000	S = (V x R) S = ($400,000 x 50%) S = $200,000 New expectation: $210,000 New acceptance: $215,000

With this analysis, plaintiff's counsel may put the new adjusted expectation value at $235,000, and the tentative acceptance value at $225,000, something just below. The defense accepted the damage values before consideration of risk, and valued the probable verdict with risk at $200,000 – based on these calculations, he estimated an adjusted expectation at $210,000, slightly above the calculated value because of the plaintiff, individually, and how well he thought she was going to appear to the jury. He put the tentative defense acceptance derived from this number at $215,000.

The expectation values between plaintiff and defendant are $25,000 apart but the tentative acceptance values are only $10,000 apart. Given the size of damages here, one would expect this to be a bridgeable gap, and if these tentative acceptance values hold through the negotiation, the case would be expected to settle.

2. *Stop sign violation, with comparative negligence component of speed.*

Defendant ran stop sign and collided with Plaintiff; plaintiff was slightly exceeding the speed limit by just a few MPH, so there will be some risk of comparative, but not much. Plaintiff estimates the probability to be 80/20. Defense estimates it at 70/30. Mid-range, non-permanent damage which Plaintiff's counsel estimates to have expectation value of $200,000. Defense thinks the damages are too high, and estimates them at $175,000. Plaintiff expects to have non-recoverable costs of $5,000. Defense considers non-recoverable costs to be negligible, and does not consider them in the calculations.

For plaintiff:	For Defendant:
S = (V x R) – C	S = (V x R)
S = ($200,000 x 80%) - $5,000	S = ($175,000 x 70%)
S = $160,000 - $5000	S = $122,500
S = $155,000	
New expectation: $155,000	New expectation: $122,000
New acceptance: $150,000	New acceptance: $130,000

With these results, the plaintiff recast the landmarks on the plaintiff's side to an adjusted expectation of $155,000, and a tentative adjusted acceptance of around $150,000. The defense might start with an adjusted expectation of $122,000 and a tentative adjusted acceptance of $130,000.

Where there is risk, the differences between the plaintiff and defendant will be greater than where there is no risk. After parties recast the landmarks as indicated, the difference between the tentative acceptance values would be around $20,000. Neither side could justify trying the lawsuit for this difference, but this is an iffy number and there are many cases that have gone to trial when the differences reach this range.

3. *Third example is a case with counterclaim.*

Plaintiff alleges breach the contract and seeks damages; defendant counterclaims for separate breaches and seeks counter damages. Claims are not mutually exclusive, so four results possible: P wins, D wins, both win and both lose.

The first task here is to estimate the chances of each of the four possible outcomes. In a balanced distribution with everything even, the distribution would be even – a 25% chance of each result. When watching any kind of dispute, we tend to pick sides, so human nature would indicate that a jury will probably favor one side or the other, with ties, whether or both sides winning or both sides losing, being the exception. In such case, a more likely even distribution would be 40% for each side and 20% to ties, perhaps 10% both win and 10% both lose.

There is no mathematical way to make the estimate, and jury research on individual verdicts will not help figure how the combination should be valued. The answer will be the lawyers' best approximation based on experience.

For this example, the lawyers estimate plaintiff will have a slight edge, and if the case could be tried 10 times, the allocation would come out that plaintiff will win outright 4 of 10, the defense will win its counterclaim outright 3 out of 10, both sides will win, with verdicts offsetting, 2 out of 10, and both sides will lose 1 out of 10. This means the plaintiff will win something 6 out of 10 times for a probability of 60% with the defense winning something – either a verdict or healthy offset against plaintiff's verdict – 5 out of 10 or a probability of 50%

If plaintiff's predicted "good-good" expectation of verdict is $100K, and plaintiff predicts that the defendant's counterclaim has a predicted negative "bad-bad" expectation of minus $55K, the allocation of probable verdicts would look like this in tabular form:

	Plaintiff	Defendant	Judgment
1	$100K	-0-	$100K
2	$100K	-0-	$100K
3	$100K	-0-	$100K
4	$100K	-0-	$100K
5	$100K	-$55K	$ 45K
6	$100K	-$55K	$ 45K
7	-0-	-$55K	-$55K
8	-0-	-$55K	-$55K
9	-0-	-$55K	-$55k
10	-0-	-0-	-0-
		Total	$325K

Average verdict from array: $325/10=$32.5K.

The defense can be expected to be more gloomy about the results, and given four variables to work with, if the defense gets carried away, the differences can be dramatic.

Skilled counsel will be aware of this, and may invite opposing counsel to discuss the combination percentages to be used, to see if there is any possibility of preliminary agreement, or at least of narrowing the differences. If no preliminary agreements can be reached, all participants need to keep especially in mind that the whole works is based upon guess work, nothing is set in concrete or forged from iron, and everything is negotiable to the end. Assume in this case that the defense accepted all of the percentages, and just disagreed with the plaintiff's damages, estimating instead an expectation of $80,000.

The negotiation calculations from both sides would look like this, where PV = plaintiff's risk free expectation, DV = defendant's risk free expectation, R= the risk, and S = settlement value of entire case:

From Plaintiff's side:	From Defense side:
S =(PV x R)-(DV x R)	S=(PV x R)-(DV x R)
S=(100K x 60%)-(55K x 50%)	S=(80K x 60%)-(55K x 50%)
S=(60K – 27.5K)	S=(48K)-(27.5K)
S= $32,500	S= $20,500
New expectations: $30,000	New expectation: $20,000
New acceptance: $25,000	New acceptance: $25,000

The $25,000 final tentative acceptance calculated by both parties here is not a verdict any jury would ever reach. The jury is either going to bring in a big verdict for the plaintiff – 6 times out of 10 times both sides figure the plaintiff will win something – and 4 out of 10 times the jury will either return a zero or a negative verdict of $55,000 on defendant's counterclaim.

Why would a plaintiff accept $25,000 when most of the time he might win up to $100,000? Because 4 times out of 10 plaintiff loses, and 3 of those times the verdict against him might get to $55,000. Why would a defendant pay $25,000 when it looks like he is going to win 50% of the time? Because when he wins, he doesn't win that much and when he loses, the roof falls in. These are business decisions, with cases being settled upon business principles; it is not about the winning here, it is about minimizing the risk and cost of potential losses.

Example: *The plaintiff's case was a huge claim for fraud and misrepresentation in the acquisition of a business that had failed. The defendant denied any fraud or misrepresentation, and counterclaimed for performance under the business acquisition agreement, under which there was a balance due of over $10 million. The case had been going on for several years, and the court finally ordered the parties into mediation. Negotiations started out over $30 million apart, across zero, with plaintiff claiming damages on its claim in excess of $20 million and the defendant denying owing anything and insisting it was entitled to the balance of the purchase price under its claim of over $11 million. The negotiations continued, through a mediator, for two days, until late in the second day the parties reached numbers that were $8 million apart, exactly equidistant from zero. Plaintiff was demanding to be paid $4 million, defendant claimed damages of $4 million. In the next two rounds, the parties moved by exactly the same amount, lowering the demands from $4 million to $2 million on each side, but keeping the zero in the exact middle.*

To emphasize here, the parties were now $4 million dollars apart. When the last move was announced, with zero still the mid-point, the main spokesman for the plaintiff's side suddenly said "OK, if that's where we are headed, so be it. If the other side will accept the zero and walk away, so will we." The other side immediately accepted, and that was that. Releases were exchanged all around, all litigation was dismissed, and the cases ended with nobody paying anybody a dime.

14
Special circumstances

Cost avoidance considerations

This is a special tool of settlement valuation, available in some cases. The cost of litigation frequently has a play in the settlement of a questionable outcome case. Litigation is enormously expensive, and most sophisticated consumers of legal services – meaning insurance companies, corporations frequently targeted for lawsuits, and the like – invariably factor their costs of litigation into their strategies for settlement purposes. Even when they say they don't, they do.

For claimants with lawyers operating under contingent fee arrangements, there can be significant costs incurred in the process that are not contingent, making similar considerations of avoided costs important and available to both sides.

This aspect does not change the value of the case under the calculations proposed above for either side. The aspect of cost avoidance may, however, provide a bridge to enable the paying party to justify paying somewhat more than what it estimated the actual values to be, or the receiving party to accept somewhat less, in recognition of the value to be realized in cutting off and avoiding the future cost of litigation.

The true utility of a cost avoidance analysis is where counsel faces the prospect of trying to settle a weak or middling in-betweener – where the predictable chances of a decent verdict on any straight line value of case analysis may be debatable. The concept is that the party on the paying end of the balance, will boost up the offer being made based on the estimates of actual value by adding to the offer a number taken from the fees and costs that will have to be paid if the case continues, but that will be saved if the case settles right now. It doesn't change the lawyer's estimate of the underlying litigation value of the case in the analysis; rather it adds an incentive to settle by recognizing a cost saving available in the process.

For example, suppose the case involves a claim where the plaintiff claims his damages exceed $200,000 adjusted value, with a 60% probability of winning, for an adjusted expectation of $120,000. Suppose defendant agrees on the risk assessment at 60% but thinks the damages are only $140,000, or an adjusted expectation of $84,000. Suppose no one is getting attorney fees as a prevailing party, so everyone is responsible for their own fees, and plaintiff is stuck on a demand of $115,000. Defendant does not want to go higher than $90,000 on its assessment of the risks.

Defense counsel estimates that it will require at least $50,000 in fees and costs to take the case from the current position through trial. He will have to spend another $50,000 in order to see if he can save the 25,000 difference between defendant's best case valuation at $90,000 and plaintiff's demand of $115,000.

Suppose instead he offers the plaintiff the $90,000 value taken by the defense from the defense top dollar acceptance value, plus adds another $25,000 – being half the estimated cost he will have to incur if he continues the case – to make a total package of $115,000. The defense can justify this addition because it is considerably less than the fixed costs of going forward. The number satisfies the plaintiff's demand, and on balance, the defense saves an estimated $25,000 in avoided costs.

What is important here is that the aspect of cost avoidance is by definition more significant to an earlier rather than a later settlement effort.

If the proposal comes too late in the course of litigation, there may not be significant costs left to be saved. Once significant fees or costs are actually incurred, any motivation for future cost avoidance begins to evaporate. In poker, this is referred to as being pot-committed; there is so much money in the pot, relative to the amount of the current wager required to stay in, that the player feels compelled to stay in the pot, regardless of the odds indicated by the cards. The same thing can happen in litigation.

Where cost avoidance – on either side – might be in play, the earlier this aspect of the settlement effort is undertaken, the better. If cost avoidance has any potential of being a factor, counsel should not defer settlement consideration of a questionable outcome case.

A second area where a cost avoidance settlement might have a play is where the case might have a significant potential jury verdict, but the case is very risky and would involves significant time and expense to obtain. A carefully phrased request by the claiming party may encourage a defending entity to make an offer based on cost avoidance to avoid litigation completely, even where the defendant may be convinced that it would win the case if suit was filed.

The author's experience with an avoided cost settlement occurred many years ago but is still instructive today.

Example: The client was a recent widow whose husband and a friend had been killed in an private airplane crash. The husband and friend had been flying a Cessna 172 that the husband owned when they unexpectedly ran into bad weather and crashed. He was a low time VFR (visual flight only) pilot; his friend was a much higher time, IFR (instrument rated) qualified pilot. It was not possible to tell who was flying the plane at the time of the crash. (The Cessna 172, like most private aircraft, has dual controls, and can be flown from either of the front seats.) The NTSB report attributed the cause to pilot error, without assigning who had been flying the aircraft at the time. After minimal investigation, it appeared there might be claims against Cessna and the aircraft repair facility that had recently overhauled the engine, because of a defective part found in the wreckage that might have allowed exhaust gases to leak into the cabin.

It would require expert analysis to confirm any of this, which would have been expensive. Even if something turned up, the case was rife with risk. If the plaintiff could prevail, the death case might have been worth as much as $300,000, which was a healthy amount for a wrongful death at the time. The insurance representative met with the author, acting as the widow's attorney, and advised that the carrier insured both Cessna and the *airframe repair facility. The carrier would offer the widow $60,000 right then for a complete release of all potential defendants – but the deal was off the table if suit was filed. The widow was advised that the death case was worth substantially more than $60,000, but that it would be very risky and very expensive to try, and would take years to complete. She took the money. The other fellow's widow elected to sue. It took three years to get her case to trial, but she did receive a handsome verdict of about $350,000.*

The author called his former client, who had moved to a distant city to rejoin her family, to see what she thought of all the developments. He learned that she was perfectly satisfied with her settlement and not concerned a bit about the verdict her friend received. She had invested her money in a business that was thriving and had grown over the years to be worth more than the verdict.

In the friend's case, the litigation continued for two more years while the parties fought through post-trial motions and then an appeal. The case finally settled on appeal for a confidential amount.

What is important here is that the aspect of cost avoidance is by definition more significant to an earlier rather than a later settlement effort.

As should be obvious, once significant fees or costs are actually incurred, any motivation for future cost avoidance will evaporate. In poker, this is referred to as being pot-committed; there is so much money in the pot, relative to the amount of the current wager required to stay in, that the relative cost of seeing the hand through, regardless of the odds indicated by the cards, does not justify folding.

The same thing can happen in litigation. Where cost avoidance – on either side – might be in play, the earlier this aspect of the settlement effort is undertaken, the better. If cost avoidance has any potential of being a factor, counsel should not defer settlement consideration of a questionable outcome case.

Early case evaluation

Ordinarily, the settlement effort will occur in the midst of active, adversarial litigation. The strong recommendation as presented earlier in this book is that settlement efforts not be considered until the case is fully prepared and ready to go. Ideally, it will be ready for trial. At a minimum, it will have progressed to the point where essential discovery has been completed, major depositions of the claiming parties have been taken, and all counsel are comfortable with the essential facts.

Occasionally, counsel will be presented with a case so clear cut and so obvious that a solution ought to be available without going to the time, effort and expense of a full work up on all facets of trial preparation. There are other situations where the next step in trial preparation will be inordinately expensive or time consuming, and the question is presented as to whether some effort at settlement might be attempted to avoid the expense and inconvenience. The question becomes, how to best set up and present a settlement situation in such a circumstance?

It is possible provided the other side agrees and provided that certain critical prerequisites exist. It can be accomplished with direct negotiation, but is particularly amenable to negotiation through a mediator. The device is an early case evaluation through mediation. The idea is a mediation before any complaint is filed, and with an informal exchange of information but no formal discovery, or early in the case before the inordinately expensive discovery is begun. Because the process contemplates a fair and thorough exchange of information without the protection of the rules, there must be a considerable amount of trust between the opposing sides.

In order for the process to work, there are three essential requirements:

- There cannot be any disagreement over any of the basic facts. The facts must be open and known, or capable of objective verification, with both sides in agreement and no open issues on any material fact. Experts are not necessary. Neither lawyer needs expert testimony to understand either their own or the other side's claims of fact; both sides can agree upon the technical aspects of the facts without the need for further expert assistance.

- While the case may be highly technical, within the technology, there are no disputes, or it can be assumed as such for purposes of the analysis; liability and any defense theories are based upon established legal precedents in the jurisdiction; everything can be put together with off-the-shelf methods without reference to any esoteric theories or futuristic extrapolations of law.
- Most important: opposing counsel must know and respect each other. The method should not be tried with unknown counsel, and time should not be wasted trying it with lawyers who are not trusted or who have questionable reputations.

All assumptions on essential facts should be reduced to writing and approved by both sides. The parties may agree that the assumptions are only for the purpose of the early case evaluation and mediation, and are not binding on nor may be used in any manner by either party if the case does not settle.

The concept of an early case evaluation and mediation means conducting mediation on the case well before it would otherwise be considered ready for the settlement effort. The concept calls for a significant cutting of corners by both sides from normal trial and settlement preparation to save money, time and effort. For example, the parties may agree that only the depositions of the injured party need be taken prior to the settlement effort. They may agree upon extent of injury and causation based upon the medical chart without resorting to expert testimony or an independent medical examination by a doctor selected by the defense. They may go with magazine articles or textbook passages for the expert opinions needed.

The nature of the case where early case evaluation might apply will seldom turn on any aspect of competing expert opinions.

Counsel would certainly retain experts to explain the case to the jury, but neither counsel needs expert assistance to understand the case themselves and they do not contemplate dueling experts for the settlement effort. The lawyers are sufficiently knowledgeable about the technology involved that they know what the experts are expected to say, and can fully accommodate the differences in their analysis without the need of bagging and tagging a pair of real experts just for settlement.

Example: *The case involved a product liability claim against the U.S. importer of a foreign car that the automatic transmission or clutch mechanism on the foreign manufactured, high-end sports sedan failed, causing the car to roll and crash, resulting in injuries to the owner-driver and his wife, who was a passenger, and in demolishing their car.*

The accident was a terrifying single car rollover at high speed, but the occupants were securely belted and suffered only moderate injuries. The only treatment was at the emergency room and a short admission for minor surgeries, with normal convalescence followed by full recovery all around with no residuals. The car was severely damaged but completely repaired, although claimant contends now it suffers the "stigma" of having been wrecked, which significantly impacts its resale value. The estimates were that the maximum recovery for the injuries sustained might reach $60,000 with some influence due to the "wow" factor of the accident, with a more probable result being in the total range of $40,000 for both claims, measured in today's dollars.

Several car magazines had articles on the problems of this particular auto, although the dynamics of the accident in this case were not exactly in line with the published reports. Counsel were at the point in the litigation where they were going to have to travel to Germany to take depositions of the manufacturing people, plus retain experts in Germany on the design and usage issues. The travel costs, expert fees, deposition costs and attorney fees involved would exceed $50,000 for both sides.

The parties agreed to a stand-down in the litigation and to an early case evaluation and mediation based up the above facts. Both sides agreed that the technical facts were as stated in the media reports, that there was a manufacturing defect in the transmission/clutch, and that expert testimony on both sides of the causation issue would be available if the case were to go to trial.

At the mediation, the defendant agreed to substitute a brand new vehicle of the same model and fittings for the then two year old original. The defense took possession of the old vehicle, and the new vehicle was simply substituted for the old in plaintiff's financing. This created a sizable equity for the plaintiffs because of the amount they had paid off on the old car and the upgrade they were getting on the new. In addition, the company paid both plaintiffs about half the expectation value of the damage claim for their injuries, to be divided between them as they saw fit. Releases all around and a dismissal of all litigation ended the lawsuit. The defense lawyer estimated that the settlement saved close to $75,000 by this early settlement in terms of avoided litigation cost in the U.S. and the expenses of the German trip for its U.S. local counsel. The new car in exchange for the old was of negligible cost to the manufacturer company.

The plaintiffs saved a huge sum in avoiding the German trip plus achieved a settlement with a value of somewhere between $40,000 and $50,000 counting the added equity in the new car. Both sides considered the early process to be a fruitful result.

What will cripple an early case evaluation is for one side or the other to decide, in the middle of the effort, that they will no longer accept some fact or technical theory because they have not seen the evidence of such and there in nothing in their file upon which to base the conclusion. If this is going to be the opponent's position just as soon as the negotiation starts to pinch a little, there is no point in trying.

Ambush tactics can also include not honoring the agreement to stand down, insisting upon additional information without reciprocation, and refusing to accept the assumptions and hypotheticals when the time comes to begin the dialogue on money.

Shutting down is perhaps more common, with the opponent suddenly uncomfortable in accepting the assumptions needed to make the thing work. If the opponent cannot be convinced to proceed without the assurances of competed discovery, the early case evaluation will fail.

Attempts at early case evaluation may also fail if the defending party equates the other side opting for this process as meaning they are willing to sacrifice the case on the cheap.

While there are considerable savings in costs and in the time factor, and the paying party may expect the receiving party to accept some discount for such, in an early case evaluation does not necessarily mean a settlement on the cheap.

Handicapping the lawyers

Experienced trial counsel routinely adjust their assessment for settlement values in particular cases based on the competence and experience levels of the attorneys representing the other side. These are invariably adjustments applied by the defense against claimant's counsel. The measurement is on two scales: First an absolute measure of the competence of the lawyer, and second a comparative measure of the opposing lawyer 's abilities and experience compared to the ability and experience of the rating party's counsel.

These are risky adjustments because the circumstances can change suddenly, sometimes leaving too little time to react and readjust or to arrange for a do-over.

The handicap adjustments, if they come at all in this area, are usually in three areas: (1) for the inexperienced, (2) for the incompetent or unprepared, and (3) for the lawyer who is in over his head.

First is the discount for the inexperienced. It is true that every lawyer has to try his first case sometime. But a brand new or inexperienced lawyer should not be surprised if it feels like the opponent is holding back in settlement offers until the newbie demonstrates his ability to survive in the courtroom. In modern litigation, it is almost essential that a lawyer's first few cases be as second chair to a seasoned litigator, and that new lawyers not attempt to go solo without a mentor hovering nearby just in case. Also, new lawyers should start out their solo ventures with simpler cases and build into the more difficult. If the new lawyer can pull it off well, he may soon find the defense coming on earlier and earlier with increasing offers. Otherwise, he will have to prove himself to a jury or two before the companies will step up.

The second handicap adjustments are subtractions for the incompetent or unprepared. Usually, it can be determined early on if counsel is not competent, or is not spending the time necessary to keep up with the case. If the lack of preparation is endemic and persistent, by the time the settlement opportunity comes along, that lawyer may find that the opposition is holding back the potential full settlement authority.

Example:

The case was a straight-forward auto accident with some chance of comparative fault. The tricky feature was some unsavory history in the plaintiff's past which may or may not be relevant. The plaintiff's lawyer was a family member, a brand new lawyer who had never tried a case before. There was an attempt at a judicial settlement conference within a month of trial that went nowhere.

It was obvious that the plaintiff's lawyer was not managing the case well, and was not prepared for the mediation, let alone any trial. He had not insisted on complete answers to interrogatories, had not filed a motion in limine to exclude the more unsavory parts of the client's past, and had left off a crucial expert. His requested jury instructions indicated a significant lack of understanding on several key issues.

Normally, the case might have been worth between \$30,000 and \$50,000, but the most that the insurance company was offering at the judicial settlement conference was \$3,500. The lawyer literally did not know what to do, and it was the plaintiff herself who declined the offer.

For an unrelated reason, the trial was vacated and reset. During the hiatus, the plaintiff, with her lawyer's support and assistance, found new counsel – an experienced plaintiff's trial lawyer. Within a week of the notice of substitution of counsel, the *defendant upped the offer from $3,500 to$35,000, and the case settled within a few days.*

The third consideration is the lawyer in over his head. It is not unusual for normally competent counsel to find himself or herself in the middle of technical litigation that is beyond his or her experience to handle.

A medical malpractice case is a prime example. These cases may appear straightforward at the outset, but the procedures required are loaded with technical booby traps set to completely derail the case and disarm the unaware. These cases are no place for the inexperienced, and if the defense realizes that the plaintiff's counsel is unfamiliar with the intricacies of medical malpractice trials and does not know what he is doing, settlement efforts may never get off the ground.

If all that is forthcoming from the defense side are low offers that are clearly well under what the case is rationally worth, and plaintiff's lawyer cannot figure out why, the reason may well be the handicap the defense has assigned to the case on account of the plaintiff's lawyer.

Any attempt to ignore the realistic boundaries of competence and experience, or to stretch those limits beyond normal growth or outside channels of expected experience, may result in deprecated settlement offers coming from the opposition. If counsel realizes the issue, prompt association with or referral to experienced counsel can usually reverse the effect. If counsel does not realize the circumstance, he or she may see only lowball offers, and when the forced trial arrives, disaster lurks. The take away here on all three areas is that the lawyer must know his or her own limits.

One thing to avoid if faced with this on the other side is the trap of lowered standards of preparation in response.

If defense counsel becomes aware that plaintiff's counsel is not up to the tasks demanded, defense counsel must exercise self-discipline to ensure that he or she does not become complacent in the face of a weak opponent. It is a frequent occasion for the adverse party to recognize the problem well before any true loss in the case has occurred, discharge the incompetent lawyer and retain new counsel who are up for the tasks demanded.

It would be a very awkward thing if defense counsel slacked off, then found himself behind an eight-ball when the plaintiffs show up on the morning of trial with new counsel, well known, competent, prepared, and ready to go.

15
Negotiation in action

All the necessary steps of due diligence and discovery in preparation for negotiation have been completed. Plaintiff's lawyers have carefully categorized the case from the standpoint of its place the matrix of overall probability of success, and predicted a realistic range of verdicts, given the risks and costs of taking the case forward. Counsel have predicted the probable outcomes of the case and calculated their aspiration and expectation landmarks and a tentative acceptance values.

As is absolutely essential before any overtures of settlement are made to the opposing side, the lawyers have carefully explained all of their findings and conclusions their clients, and have made sure that they and their clients are in complete agreement on the findings, evaluations, and conclusions so far. If the client is not in agreement or does not understand, the lawyers were prepared to loop back to the problem areas and work it through again. They would step it clear back to the basics, if need be, and forward to the present. And again if needed. The client must agree upon the strategies and upon the foundation parts the lawyers intend to use. The clients have done so.

The case is ready for negotiation. A mediator is selected. A discussion with clients and counsel have resolved exactly who will attend the mediation, which lawyers will attend, and who will lead for the plaintiffs.

The mediation is convened

The lawyers, with their clients' concurrence, make the decision of whether to negotiate directly with the opposition or work through a mediator. The decision was made to work through a mediator. A mediator is selected, and an agreement is reached for both sides to gather in the conference rooms of defense counsel to participate in the settlement effort. Everyone expected to be there is present.

For the purpose of the explanations to follow, the process will be a negotiation through a mediation. But exactly the same strategies, tactics and moves discussed and explained here would apply to a direct negotiation. Also, the discussions and explanations are largely from the plaintiff's side. To get the defense perspective, step through the glass and imagine the same element from the opposite side.

One of the advantages of a mediation is that the mediator will be there as a coach or teacher or guide to explain all this to the participants as they work through the moves. In direct negotiation, the exact same strategies and tactical decisions arise, but counsel will have to remember what the moves are, what the meanings are, how to interpret them, and how to apply the information gleaned to responses. As in everything, experience matters and practice counts; the first couple of times out, if counsel does not want to use a mediator, counsel should associate an experienced negotiator to keep things in line.

Once the negotiation is convened and everybody is physically present, that does not mean that all are "connected." In fact, they are probably not. It is usually several rounds before the necessary parties are all actually plugged into the process, and ready to make progress.

The opening session with a mediator is primarily just to introduce everybody and have the mediator explain how the process will work. In the early days of mediation, both sides were allowed to give opening statements, but this proved to be not only unnecessary but counterproductive. The opening statements were invariably adversarial, often inflammatory, and served only to antagonize the opponents. In modern times, the opening session is little more than a "meet and greet," with the opportunity to see exactly who is present on both sides. The mediator may have taken a few minutes to explain the process to everyone, and he may have a few clarifying questions to ask of the lawyers, but will rarely ask anybody to give a speech. Very soon, in a general litigation mediation session where the intent is to conduct a distributive negotiation dialogue, the group will be divided up, with each side assigned to its own room. The mediator will move back and forth between the rooms with the mediation messages – the two sides will not communicate directly.

In direct negotiation, the participants – usually the lawyers – will communicate directly across a table, with breaks to caucus among themselves or with their client if needed. Or more commonly, the lawyers will communicate by telephone, hanging up between each bid or response, to confer and consult. No matter what the processes, and whether direct or through mediation, the pieces and parts are all the same.

The connection

Two issues are involved here: Who should make the opening offer and what should it be? There is a lot of strategy that can go into the answers to these questions.

Any words spoken at the beginning of the process can constitute an "opening offer" whether there is any thought behind it or not. There is a distinction between opening the negotiation with any number and opening with a meaningful offer. Although there may be permutations off of this theme, there are three basic moves in the opening. Two are "meaningful" and one is not.

- A "responsive offer" is a meaningful offer. It is a number or value that is intended to connect the parties to the negotiation and carry the dialogue forward. It is intended to be relevant to both sides. It is a declaration, or the beginning of a declaration, of where the maker of the offer expects the final ballpark to be. This may sound like a lot of "oomph" to put into one number, but in actual practice it is surprising how much information is conveyed by a carefully crafted negotiation move. If the responsive offer is the first offer of the series, it is said to be the "anchoring offer," a term coined by the Harvard Negotiation Project to denote the first meaningful offer in a negotiation.

- A "relevant offer" is a meaningful offer. It is a number that is relevant to the maker but not necessarily to the respondent. It is not of the character of an anchoring offer. Frequently this will be an offer that is tied to the maker's "aspirations" value of the case. It is intended to convey that the maker is serious about the negotiation, attentive and interested in the process, but defers any commitment to value until more information is presented from the other side.
- A "random offer" is not meaningful. It is a number that is not connected to anything relevant, nor to any feature within reach of the case under any construction of the facts. If it comes in the middle of the case, it is an "off the wall" number that is disconnected from anything that preceded it. It is not responsive and not considered productive. If it comes in the beginning, it conveys nothing meaningful about the case, and merely serves to pass the move to the other side.

When the plaintiff is making the opening move, and there have been no discussions of settlement prior to the mediation, the plaintiff's lawyers may not want to step out too far before they learn where the defense will be coming from. To keep their hand totally concealed, the plaintiffs may open with a "random" number.

There is nothing wrong with starting a negotiation with a random number; it happens many times, and is a legitimate device to mark time while other parties are struggling with the connection phase, or to pass the responsibility (and the opportunity) of making the real "opening offer" over to the other side. Although not a usual tactic, it can also be used in the middle of a negotiation, if there is a necessity for a non-committal message – sort of like a pause in the process.

Amount of opening offer

It does not matter who is chosen to speak first. What does matter is whether the party chosen wants to make a controlling or relevant offer, or would prefer to pass the baton to the other side and let them decide the opening strategy. If the party decides that it does not want to show its hand this early and would prefer to let the other side commit first, it simply makes a "random offer," not connected to anything, or perhaps a "relevant offer" which demonstrates interest and alertness but provides no insight into values, both of which serve only to pass the opportunity to the other side.

While a random number can be anything, from a practical standpoint, the random number should not be too distant from the range of numbers expected to be used in the case. It is a waste of time to start with a "pie in the sky" number that is very, very large, and way out of range of the values estimated for the real case. The opposing side will not be discomfited by a huge number; they will respond with numbers to mark time – random numbers of their own, or relevant numbers that move sideways and make no progress – so long as the opening bidder is not being realistic. Putting a pie in the sky up as the opening offer serves only to delay actual progress on the case until the values are brought down to the expected range.

Example: *The case was a horrific truck jackknife that wiped out three passenger vehicles, killing the three drivers. Three wrongful death cases ensued that were remarkably similar. In each, the decedent was the family breadwinner, professional and well-to-do, and the only occupant of the vehicle; survivors were the spouse and minor children plus one dependent adult family member in each case – a handicapped sibling in one case and an aged parent in the other two; all three decedents were of approximately the same age and economic status. The cases were separately filed by separate counsel, but combined for a mediation. Separate plaintiff's counsel for each case, the three surviving widows, plus Idaho counsel for the truck carrier, and a national claims specialist who specialized in truck disasters made up the mediation participants. The mediator was a retired judge.*

The opening demands were in the range of $4.0 million from the first plaintiff, $3.6 million from the second and $23 million from the third. Within about five hours, the first two cases settled, *one for about $1.9 million and the other for about $2.2 million. Three hours later the third settled for $2.1 million. The only thing accomplished by the $23 million pie-in-the-sky opening was to extend the mediation by about three hours.*

A “relevant” offer is a number attached to something relevant to the case from the offering side, but not necessarily responsive to anything from the opposing side. The total damage calculation provided to the other side, for example, or that total minus a specific element. Or it is the party’s aspiration value. But it won’t have all the “oomph” of an anchoring opening offer. It does not contain within it the commitment of the maker to the process, any recognition of the other side’s position, or the declaration of expected range. It is simply a number that is not random.

Usually, the anchoring offer will come from the party with the most knowledge about the case. Another way of looking at it is that the anchoring offer will usually come from the party that has the least to prove. In the abstract, this will usually be the paying party, usually the defendant, since the claiming party, usually the plaintiff, has the burden of proof and the one expected to pay may be entitled to sit back and wait. Also, the only party with real money in the game is the defendant. The plaintiff’s numbers may look like money, but in reality they are nothing but flashy lures meant to attract the defendant out of its lair. While both parties may have equal knowledge of the facts, only the defendant brought real money to the room and only the defendant knows how much of it is going to be put up in settlement.

While this is usually the case, it is not always so. In an admitted liability case, for example, where the damages are virtually certain, or a drunken misconduct case, where the jury may be horrified, it may actually be the defendant who has to disprove the plaintiff’s entitlement to the damages claimed, and the plaintiff who must be satisfied with the money put up, making the plaintiff the one with the “least to prove” in damages and in best position to make the anchoring offer.

This is not a hard and fast rule, as in the long run it does not matter who makes the anchoring offer. In fact, it is not uncommon to see both sides make anchoring offers, and then even to repeat them until one side emerges as the one having better control over the process.

In the truck disaster illustration, the two smaller starting demands one for $4.0 million and the other for $3.6 million, were thought to be relevant openings, probably in the vicinity of the parties' aspirations. The defense response in the range of $500,000 was an anchoring move. In both cases, the end result was fairly close to the midpoint initially established by the $500,000 opening.

The response to the opening demand of $23 million was $23,000 – clearly considered to be a random move by the defendant. It took several hours, and a number of random moves on both sides, before an anchor offer was finally tendered in this case, and real progress was finally initiated.

Importance of control

Much is written about control of a negotiation including advice on how to seize control, how to maintain control, and how to get it back if it is lost. It may make a difference in *integrative negotiation* where the parties may be concerned with "looking outside the box" and "expanding the pie" and otherwise searching for creative solutions. But in the case of *distributive negotiation* to a hard money value, it does not make any difference who has control. The responding party has plenty of protection, and nothing is going to happen without everyone's acceptance. In a direct negotiation, it is not unusual to see control of the process pass back and forth as the negotiators move through the phases.

In mediation, the mediator will appear to have control as an incident of his control of the process, and will appear to defer equally to each side in their caucus as to substantive control.

The only real significance is that the controlling party will usually be the one to advance the meaningful offers for the responding party to consider; will propose the direction and pace of movement toward the ballpark; will initiate change in direction or pace when indicated and when acceptable; and will signal, if needed, the turn and the approach to close. The non-controlling party usually keys its replies as responses to the controlling offer. Occasionally, the reply will also constitute a counteroffer, intended to offer to take the negotiation in a new direction, Especially early in a mediation or direct negotiation, where there is uncertainty about the relative positions of the parties, control may appear to be passed back and forth as the parties appear to test their different approaches to settlement.

Eventually and usually, the party expected to pay will take control and guide the negotiation. Here, it is an adjunct of the "Golden Rule of Negotiation" – he who brings the gold makes the rules. If it is going to work, it doesn't make any difference.

Setting the pace

Once a meaningful opening offer is on the table, all further moves will either be "random," "relevant" or "responsive." The meanings now should be obvious. The "random" reply signifies nothing; it is neither relevant nor responsive, but merely serves to pass the move back to the other side. The "relevant" move is relevant, but not responsive. Finally, the "responsive" reply is relevant and responsive. The basic message unit in any negotiation is an exchange, which is an offer coupled with a reply. Each reply also constitutes a new offer, and the process continues with consecutive replies.

The negotiation process is said to have moved on out of the "convening phase" and into the "connection phase" when both sides have introduced offers that are at least "relevant", i.e., offers that indicate interest and intent, albeit without commitment. The negotiation is out of the "connection phase" and into the "exploration phase" when both sides introduce "responsive" moves; i.e., two consecutive exchanges including responsive replies from both sides.

The objective of a successful negotiation is to link together a series of exchanges, starting with the anchoring offer at the opening and continuing without a break until they reach home plate. This means that ideally, all the moves will be responsive

Usually, the party making the anchoring offer will control the pace of the mediation as it moves into the exploration sessions. There is no particular tactical advantage to being the control party versus the responding party. It is simply the nature of the process that the paying party usually makes the anchor offer and usually controls the pace of the negotiation. The responding party is not disadvantaged in any way. This party has plenty of tools to make its wishes and intentions known to the other side, and the case will not settle until both parties are completely satisfied.

As the negotiation moves through exploration phase, the party in control will advance a series of offers to see what the reaction is from the responding party. The response will signal whether the responding either approves or disapproves of the last movement – or remains neutral. With that information in mind, the anchoring party makes adjustments if necessary and advances another test offer, and the process repeats. In an uneventful negotiation, this process may continue without delay or detour until both parties are in the ballpark and ready to make their turn to home plate.

The release of rationality

It is typical to find that in the early rounds, all the moves are directly related to values claimed by that party's side, without regard to the opposition moves.

Plaintiff's opening move states, "We'll settle this case for $77,263.55," being a number to the exact penny that contains totals of itemized special damages to the penny. The next round, counsel may say, "We will drop the invoices from the western hospital for the diagnostic testing and reduce the employment claim by 10% and therefore take $64,235.25," and so forth, with each move tied to specific amounts and specific deductions. While relevant, these moves say nothing about the opposing position, or about the ultimate settlement value of the case, and are probably not "responsive."

It is a clear signal that the party is moving beyond merely "connecting" to the process , and is seriously engaged in the "exploration" for a solution when that party's moves signal a recognition of the opponent's position. An unmistakable indication of that is where the party's move loses the exact measure of damage down to the penny, and states the offered value as a rounded number somewhere in the middle of the target path towards the ballpark. Where the moves are intended to no longer be rationally attached to the early values, but rather responsive to the offers from the opposition, the numbers will lose that specificity.

This is significant because for a true commitment to settlement to happen, both sides must abandon their attempts to keep a rational attachment between their current position and their original tabulation of values and recognize that the eventual settlement value will have to include a combination of both parties' values, without a specific reference to either. The final result will just be a number that is somewhere in the middle.

One way of telling when a party has moved their head to this place, and away from their original values is when the party stops making its adjusting move specific to the dollar, or sometimes to the penny, and begins making their adjusting moves in round numbers. In the above example, the plaintiff in the next round may say, "Well drop our demand from $64,235.25 to $58,000." Bingo! Losing the specificity is incontrovertible proof that the party has finally moved into the "exploration" stage and is committed to trying to find a settlement number.

No guarantee of success yet, but it's not going to be for want of a serious try.

Preserving the split-value move

Once the parties have dropped the justification of attaching each move back to specific values in their original computation, and have begun stating the negotiation bids in round numbers, the moves should stay with a consistent level of round numbers selected.

If, for example, the moves transfer into numbers rounded to a nearest thousand, keep all subsequent moves in numbers to full thousands; if the level is nearest hundred, keep all subsequent moves in full hundreds. Be consistent in this level of accuracy until it is time to send a signal that the final value is near.

This means that if on the next round, someone wants to go to $47,500, and it's not close to the last round yet, the mediator would insist that the move be either $47,000 or $48,000, and that the split-value be reserved as a signal to send later.

The middle ground

The signals with real meaning come with the subsequent moves off the anchor. It's the second and third number, taken in context with the anchor, which become more important as a combined signal than just the opening number in isolation, or any of the subsequent numbers in isolation.

This only applies to responsive exchanges from a relevant move. If there is a random insertion, one must start over with a collection of two or three completed exchanges off of a new relevant move before attempting to ascertain the message from the combination.

Transparency

As in many card games, there is a time for the players to hold their cards close and there is a time to allow everyone to see what they have.

A certain amount of camouflage may be acceptable early in the mediation, while the negotiators are feeling each other out and seeking to ensure that the parties and counsel are all "connected" to the effort. But once the parties are connected, and certainly once into the "exploration" stage and the search for the ballpark begins in earnest, the best practice is to be transparent in the dialogue. Let the numbers selected declare firmly, accurately and *unambiguously* where counsel believes the negotiation should be headed.

If it is direct mediation, and the lawyers are exchanging banter along with the signals, care must be taken that the words of the patter are consistent with the message contained in the numbers. In a negotiation to value, the numbers should always speak louder than words, and counsel should face stiff argument if he tries to make it work otherwise. But words do matter, and the wrong words can get in the way if the speaker is not careful.

Keeping track

The negotiator should prepare a table of some kind and keep track of each bid made as the negotiation moves along. In addition to the numbers exchanged in each bid, there are three derived numbers to keep track of as a negotiation dialogue matures: (1) the midpoint between the competing bids at the end of each exchange: (2) the Delta, or the difference between the current positions of both parties, and (3) the rate of change from the last bid to this bid by each party on each move and of equal importance, whether that rate is increasing, decreasing or remaining constant. These derived figures each have specific uses at various stages of the negotiation.

Midpoint: Early in the mediation, the midpoint is a general indication of where the ballpark might be, based upon current moves, if there is no change to any patterns. Once inside the ballpark, the midpoint is an indication of where home plate is, based on current moves, if there is no change to any patterns. One the parties make the turn and head for home plate, the midpoint is an indication of the precise amount needed to settle the case.

If the parties are hinking and jinking with random moves, the midpoint will jump around with each move, and any messages will be difficult to decipher. But after a few exchanges, some relevant patterns should begin to appear. The strongest sign, is where the parties settle into a steady pattern of moves converging on a steady midpoint.

The Differential or Delta value: This value is the difference between the opposing positions after each exchange. It becomes increasingly significant as a predictor as the parties' positions converge. When the parties are some distance apart, a positive increase move is usually not greater than 25% of the Delta – if the opponent does not respond favorably, the bidder can readjust if the move was in the range of 25% or less. If a bidder makes too large a move relative to the Delta, and the responder does not reciprocate, the bidder may have to scramble to readjust. If he has moved too far too fast, the readjustment may be awkward.

Once the parties are in the ballpark, a Delta that is less than total litigation cost if the parties were to go to trial is a predictor that the case will settle. When the Delta becomes less than one side's cost of going to trial, settlement is almost a sure thing. The economics dictate that not settling the case has become too expensive. This is not an invitation to try to be greedy. Counsel cannot suddenly decide to go backwards or ring in a host of previously unmentioned conditions. The whole thing could still blow up in a heartbeat. It is very important that the Delta continues to close in a deliberate fashion as the parties converge.

It is an extremely risky sign if the Delta suddenly increases over the last moves very late in the process because a responding party suddenly pulls up sharply. A mediation will fold up in a blink if one side believes the opponent is trying to get cute, or take advantage of them, or manipulate the game.

Rate of change: The rate of change is the differential between a party's last move and the current move, and can carry a ton of information. The information one gleans from the rate of change is (a) whether there is any pattern to the rate and if so, whether the pattern is (b) in relation to the opponent's moves or (c) derived independently of the adversary's moves. Further, if there is a pattern, is the pattern (d) changing, and if changing, whether it is (e) increasing or (f) decreasing. Reading the message intended by a change in the pattern of moves is an art, but a necessary art.

The mediator can be invaluable here in either decoding the meaning of the message or just plain explaining the message from what was told to the mediator by the opponent. One of a mediator's functions is to ensure that the negotiation messages passed back and forth are not misunderstood.

16
Constructing the bids

Negotiation bids

The “bid” in a negotiation is an offer to pay or offer to accept a given dollar figure in settlement of the case. The bid may be either direct or indirect. The direct move is where the value of the bid is declared in the bid itself. Indirect moves are where the value of the real bid is derived or inferred from the values declared in the bid offered.

An “exchange” is a bid coupled with a response. The exchange is the basic unit of measurement in a negotiation. A bid in isolation is meaningless. It only has meaning when measured by the response it elicits. The objective in a negotiation is to establish a linked chain of relevant exchanges extending from the beginning positions of each party to home plate.

Direct moves in a negotiation can be random, pattern, mirror or ratio. Random moves have been defined, and are just what the label says. A pattern move is any series of moves constructed as an independent pattern, without reference to the opposition’s move. Mirror and ratio moves are responsive moves, and take their meaning from the opposition’s move.

Pattern moves are a series of independent moves, establishing a pattern within the series of moves but not in response to the opposition moves.

- If the pattern is a decreasing series, that is usually a signal that the maker is slowing down. Either the opponent is not closing fast enough and needs to increase the bids, or the bidder is getting close to their stopping place.

- A pattern that is an increasing series, but not in relation to opposition moves, is seeking a move that is intended to spark the opponent into action. The opponent is making tiny, random moves that are way too high or way too low.
- A constant pattern is series of identical moves made without reference to what the opposing move is until the end, but progressing towards the area of the ballpark in a series of even steps. The hallmark of the step move is that no modifications of the step in response to the plaintiff's moves are made until the plaintiff is within a range that is approximately equidistant from the objective. The author's pet name for this pattern is the "insurance adjuster's shuffle."

A pattern does not give anything away about where the bidder is headed or what value he expects until he reaches his goal.

Mirror moves are bids that are identical to the opponent's last bid. It is a very strong, positive move in negotiation, conveying satisfaction with rate of change, the converging difference, and the value of the midpoint. A mirror response can be adjusted slightly and still retain its character as a mirror move. A slight move up is a progressive move. This signals satisfaction with the general approach and invites an increase in the incremental value to step up the speed of closure.

This is a cautious move and may be reversed next round if not received as hoped. A slight move down is a slightly negative response. It is not shutting down, as might be a move that drops by a precipitous amount, but it is expressing some degree of caution. Usually, the feature is obvious – it may be that the other side has slowed down for no reason or has changed the tempo of movement without warning the plaintiff. It indicates some degree of displeasure, but not a large measure. It is a tweak, or a poke in the ribs. A wake up call, if read correctly.

If the mediation is moving in the right direction and at a good pace, both sides may use mirrored moves with slight adjustments to fine tune the progress and shape ever so slightly the location of the midpoint coming up, while still keeping everything moving. In the best of cases, once it is clear that both parties have stopped fiddling and are marking the moves as straight mirrors, the midpoint that is then indicated will be the final destination to settlement.

In the more practical case, the parties will not actually be seen to agree upon this midpoint until very late in the process, as they both will still want to try to weight the result with their own values. Usually, it will not be until the final rounds that the exact finish can be predicted. Timing here is critical.

Ratio moves are responsive moves in some ratio to the opposition move and in reference to the midpoint. Early in the dialogue, ratios can be used to suggest where a suitable ballpark will be after given number of moves; later in the dialogue, ratio moves will suggest a final midpoint to aim at for the final goal. A series of ratio bids will shift the midpoint to the desired location in an identifiable and uniform number of moves, when the bidders start out from unequal distances away the desired target.

For example, assume the parties start with the defense at 0 and the plaintiff at 1,000 chips, with the targeted objective being 300 chips. At 0, the defense is 300 chips away from this target, and at 1,000 the plaintiff is 700 away. If the plaintiff moves first, and drops down 100 to 900 chips, what should the defense move be so that both will reach 300 at the same time, if the plaintiff continues to drop 100 each time? Answer: at 100 moves, if will take plaintiff 7 moves to go from 1,000 to 300. If defendant covers the distance to 300 from his starting place at 0, the moves would be 3/7 or 42.86, rounded to 43.

Here's the table:

Pltf	Def	Midpoint
1,000	0	500
900	43	472
800	86	443
700	129	415
600	172	386
500	215	358
400	258	314
300	301	300

The ratio of the defense distance to the plaintiff distance, where the parties start at 0 and 1,000, is 300:700 or 3:7. To construct a dialogue where the bids will uniformly converge upon the value of 300 with plaintiff to move first, each defense move will be 3/7 of the plaintiff's move.

As shown above, where the plaintiff's move is 100 chips down, the calculated defense move is 3/7 of that number, or 43 up; if the plaintiff offer is 200 chips down, the ratio reply would be 3/7 of 200, or approximately 86 up. If the plaintiff changes its move, the defense reply will always be 3/7 of whatever move the plaintiff makes. Ratio moves will operate to cause both parties to converge on the desired targeted value uniformly, so they will arrive together, in the same number of moves.

It is not necessary to be this precise in ratio move. It is not common to design a ration series to move all the way to the targeted midpoint. More common is for the party desiring to move the midpoint to figure out by trial and error a series of moves that will place both parties within a range close to target midpoint a given number of moves, and then to make an adjusting move at the end to clarify the intent.

For example, suppose the plaintiff starting at 1000 moves down by 150, and defense starting at 0, wants to center the midpoint at 300. Defense may decide to put himself equal distant from the desired point at 300 when plaintiff reaches any value within 400 – i.e., defense to be at 200 or more if plaintiff reaches 400 or less, indicating a midpoint of 300, with 4 moves to be the trial start, since 4x150 will place the plaintiff at 400.

This easy calculation is 200/4=50, meaning defense measured move is 50 moves up for 4 moves. Plaintiff will be at 400 (1000-(4x150)=400), and defendant will be at 200 (4x50=200). The parties can now mirror each other if the intent is to settle at 300. If plaintiff makes any other move other than 150, the response is 3/7 of that move.

Here's the table:

Pltf	Def	Midpoint
1,000	0	500
850	50	450
700	100	400
550	150	350
400	200	300

Once at 400 and 200, either side can shift to mirror moves from there to the conclusion,

Ratio moves can be used any time there is a disproportionate separation between the positions of each party with respect to the midpoint target objective. Through use of the ratio moves, the parties begin to close the distance between their positions at a predicted pattern rate, while steadily moving the midpoint toward the target goal, so that the pattern can continue all the way to convergence.

Usually, ratio moves are not continued for long. Once opponent recognizes the ratio contained in the pattern of moves, and desires to accept where the pattern moves are pointing, that side can make an adjusting move, sometimes in a single jump, sometimes spread over several moves, to reset the midpoint so that the parties are equidistant. Once that occurs and is confirmed, the moves will usually become straight mirrors.

The objective in these exploratory moves is to navigate the landscape until both parties are exactly equidistant from the midpoint, where both parties can begin making mirror moves to converge.

Tactical planning

Suppose plaintiff starts with a bid of 1,000 when the defense expects the final midpoint to be in the range of 300. The defense has three tactical alternatives to respond to this initial opening. (1) wait and see, (2) start a pattern, or (3) try a ratio.

(1) *The wait and see move* is either a pure random or a relevant move that is intended just to mark time and see where the other side is heading. A very small defense opening indicates that the plaintiff's start is considered way too high. In the example, where the plaintiff is at 1,000 with 300 being the acceptable target, the defense may start with a tiny move of 10 chips or less. This gives the defense more room for a responsive signal once the plaintiff begins to respond.

An opening move that is more sufficient shows that the plaintiff's start is considered a positive step and the defense is interested and attentive. For example, if the opening bid had been in the range of 500 to 600, with 300 as the target, the defense may indicate this by a more sufficient response to 60 to 75 chips. As soon as the plaintiff drops below 500, the defense can begin with mirrors above 100.

A substantial reply move is indicative of interest in closing quickly upon values already in sight; it will usually be a move within range of the midpoint so that mirror moves can be introduced. Suppose the plaintiff starts with a move of 450. There is no point in a "wait and see" unless the defense wants to play games. The defense may immediately start with 150, and then exchange mirror moves to point to the target of 300.

In all three cases, the plaintiff's next responsive move will be most revealing and important.

(2) *To start and maintain a constant pattern*, defense selects a number that will move the defense into or within close range of the ballpark in 6 to as many as 10 moves, or so. The tactic is to then continue making this pattern move, no matter what the response, until the defense either reaches his interim target near or in the ballpark, or until the plaintiff comes within a range where mirror moves can be introduced. In the example above, the defense may select 30 chips as its pattern move, and then simply make that move every time, no matter what the plaintiff's response is, until it reaches 300, when it announces this value to be the last and final bid. The constant pattern keeps rigid control

in the defense hands, but it is the least responsive method to messages and signals from the opposition.

In the most aggressive model, the constant pattern is continued right to the bidder's final acceptance and then stops, without any warning, and without any acknowledgment of plaintiff's moves at all. The defense announces the last move as final, and that's is it. It is plaintiff's offer to accept or leave. In the more common version, the defense bidder changes tactics when the pattern bids reach the ballpark within range of the plaintiff. If the plaintiff is within range, the exchanges become more responsive. If the plaintiff is not at or within close range when the defense nears the ballpark, a re-examination is probably in order; something might be wrong.

(3) *A ratio move* is purely a responsive move; to set it up, defense will first make a relevant opening sufficient to show attention and interest, and will then key the ratio moves off of the plaintiff's responses. With the plaintiff at 1,000, and the target at 300, the defense may start with a move of 50 to invite a sufficient move from plaintiff. Depending upon plaintiff's reply, the defense can establish a ratio move applied to plaintiff's move to bring the parties to an acceptable ballpark in the vicinity of 300. If plaintiff responds with 900, for example, being a drop of 100, and defense decides appropriate boundaries would be 200 and 400, centering on 300 as the targeted midpoint, the calculations for the ratio move by the defense would work out as follows:

Description	Defendant	Plaintiff
Position at Start	50	900
Position at end	200	400
D = difference	150	500
N = moves	5	5
D/N = value of move	30	100

Indirect moves

Indirect moves are protective moves intended to offer a new position to the opponent in a negotiation dialogue, different from the current position or series, but without risking being placed at a disadvantage to respond if the opponent does not accept.

Most common here is the "conditional brackets" move. The format of the move is to couple a brackets offer with a very small direct move, as in, "Our direct move is to X, but we will move our offer to Y if you move your response to Z," where X is a small move if the conditional is not accepted, and Y and Z are the intended new position of the parties if the conditional is accepted.

If accepted, the intended effect of the move is to reset the midpoint in one jump –and to reset the dialogue to the values bounded by the brackets and centered upon the new midpoint. The real value intended to be communicated by this move is the new midpoint. It is a clear signal that this midpoint would be an acceptable objective. If early in the negotiation, it is a suggestion that this new midpoint would be somewhere near the center of the ballpark. If late in the negotiation, it is a suggestion that this would be an acceptable settlement value.

For example, assume the parties started out very far apart: defense at 0 and plaintiff at 1,000 chips. The defense knows that the case should probably settle around 350, but neither side has made any meaningful moves to close the gap, and both are stuck very close to their starting points, say 10 or 12 point off the initial margins.

The defense suggests new brackets by making a formal move of a few chips, say to 15 chips, with the added proviso, "… but we will move to 200 if you drop to 500." If the plaintiff accepts, the parties are at 200 and 500, with the new midpoint at 350. If the plaintiff does not accept, the defense has only moved to 15 and it is the plaintiff's turn to move.

It is possible to conduct the entire negotiation with "conditional bracketed" moves, where nobody mentions the settlement number until the very last move.

In the example above, the plaintiff could respond, "We will accept the move to 500 if you move to 300," to which the defense might respond, "The 300 move is acceptable to us if you move to 400," to which the plaintiff says, "We will take the 400 if you take 325," and the defense finishes with, "That 325 is acceptable to us if you go to 375." Suddenly, the parties are in the end game, each within 25 chips of the targeted value and neither one has made a formal move, value should be 350. The table would look like this:

Pltf	Def	Midpoint
1,000	0	500
995	13	504
988	15*/[200/500]	*350
*[300/500]	*[300/400]	*350
*[400/325]	*[375/325]	*350
*[375/340]	*[360/340]	*350
???		

Of course, the case is about to settle, because on the brackets, the parties are only 20 chips apart with 350 in the middle. There may be some power plays to jiggle the final ending a little bit one way or the other, but nobody can afford to litigate over these differences. But if it should fall apart now, the parties' last actual bids in the dialogue are back with the defense at 15 and 988. The "conditional brackets" move can be made at any time with the caution that the message being sent is that the inferred number in the middle is at or very close to a value that will be acceptable to the offering party as the settlement value of the case. If the move is accepted, and the offering party then wants to try to create a different midpoint or different settlement value than was inferred by the conditional brackets, confusion and distrust may well result.

A second type of indirect move is the "conditional acceptance," which is used to close the deal. The parties are standing on home plate but neither wants to make a final offer, for fear it will simple evoke a response to split the difference and cause one more round.

Say, for example, the parties are at 325 chips and 375 chips, with it obvious that 350 is the target. Plaintiff could offer to split the difference at 350, but a tightfisted defendant could respond with an offer to split the split at 337.5. Rather than risk another round with the plaintiff poorly placed to respond, the plaintiff may make a formal bid just a few chips off 375, then add, "But if you offer to split the difference at 350, we will accept."

The "conditional acceptance" does not have to be to a split, it can be to any value: "If you offer to pay X, we will accept." If the defense does anything other than accept the offer, the plaintiff's actual offer is still close to 375, and he is well placed to respond.

Conclusion

In both the planning at the outset, and the tactics employed as the negotiation progresses, the objective should be to become increasingly transparent as long as the negotiation is progressing in a positive fashion.

In the best of cases, all parties will be able to see exactly where the ending is and how to get there, and will then be able to accomplish it smoothly and without hiccups or ambush along the way.

17
Buttoning up

Once the parties have explored the ballpark and identified home plate, and are satisfied that it is home plate, the negotiation dialogue will change gears again. The parties will make the turn and head for home.

The tenor of the mediation will change. The moves will be more precise, and in narrower ranges. If the general bids have been in increments of rounded thousands, the moves after the turn may be in increments of one hundred, or even less.

Usually, since the defendant is the one with the money, the plaintiff will want the defense to make the last move, and to declare that it is the last move. If the defense accepts the plaintiff's last move, the plaintiff will always wonder if he set the move too low – if he had asked for a little more, if he could have got it.

Because of this, and although the midpoint may appear to be obvious, the claiming party will still aim a little high – but not too high. The claiming party wants the paying party to empty their purse; they want everything that is in it down to the very last nickel and the lint that is clinging to it. To get this, the claiming party's moves are bait, which has to be placed very close to and just above the paying party's nose, but not too far away. There should be no chance of leaving any loot in the paying party's purse.

Empty all pockets

A significant step that has to be taken at the turning point is for everybody with any claim to the pot to empty their pockets. This means to get up and out in the open any additional terms or any extra conditions that will be expected if the case is to settle, in addition to the yet to be agreed upon sum of money. Unless it is already incorporated into the offers that are being passed back and forth, anything – any condition or any requirement – in addition to the payment of money that one side or the other is going to expect should be brought up no later than the initial moves at the turning point.

Of frequent concern are confidentiality and non-disparagement clauses in the final agreements.

A first reaction should be to try to talk the requesting side out of it. These clauses are difficult to write, difficult to monitor, and difficult to enforce. If what is intended is a simple anti-bragging clause, here may be no resistance to bringing this out at the turn. But if the case is a high profile lawsuit, with celebrities or significant figures in the community involved, and a complete confidentiality and non-disparagement agreement with a true claw-back provision is needed, this requirement must come much earlier than the turn. This needs to come out when the parties are defining the scope of the deal way up in the early rounds, or maybe even as part of the convening.

Example: in a wrongful termination of employment case, the young woman claimed she had been exposed to a hostile work environment and unwanted sexual advances by a supervisor, making the elements of a quid pro quo case of discrimination. She complained to the ombudsman through human resources, but received no respite. Finally, she quit, and sued for constructive discharge. The allegation of wrong doing within her department were compelling and messy, and the internal policies to catch and prevent were inadequate. At a mediated settlement, the parties worked for most of the day to come to a handsome settlement of all claims. As everything was being buttoned up, and the mediator was writing out a terms sheet for the parties, lead counsel for the employer announced, "Of course we will need a confidentiality agreement here." It was the first time this had been mentioned. "Of course we will not," the plaintiff's counsel immediately replied, "there was nothing mentioned in the *agreement we just made about confidentiality." The mediation continued for an additional hour and half before the parties finally agreed that an additional $50,000 would be added to the amount agreed upon as consideration for the confidentiality agreement. From a realistic standpoint, if the confidentiality requirement had been brought out earlier, it probably would have been accepted as part of the original handsome settlement, without the need for the addition consideration.*

The conditions to be brought out at the turn are usually closing details, and perhaps the expectation that the financial terms of settlement are nobody's business, and that no one will object to a confidentiality/non-disparagement clause without specific penalties, just to seal the deal. Also included here will be the exact timing for the payment of any money. If nothing is said, the usual assumption is that all money will be paid in cash and in full on the date close.

Where an institutional entity, large corporation, insurer, or the like is involved, the close of the settlement should be fixed within a week or two – three at the most. Occasionally, where complicated cases involving large sums are resolved, or where the loss involves excess reinsurers or coverages from Lloyds of London, extra time may be required to assemble the pot. Where private parties or smaller entities are involved, and some arrangements may have to be made to get the money together, the "furniture store rule" might be applied – "90 days is same as cash." Whenever any delay is going to be required for the party to assemble the payment, this needs to be brought out; it should never be a surprise after an apparent agreement is reached.

If longer periods of time are going to be required, or special circumstances exist, the discussions need to include the terms that are required, including collateral, interest rates, mode of payment and the like. It will be a difficult and tense negotiation if these discussions occur after one side accepted the deal thinking it was for cash to be paid immediately.

Mediator's fee in settlement

It is not uncommon for the plaintiff's side to propose a shift in the payment of the mediation fees.

This is still somewhat controversial; some mediators and some insurance companies refuse to consider any change to the agreement made at the outset. Others are perfectly willing to talk about anything that will help bring the ends together. Plaintiffs may be expected to ask that the defense pick up the tab for the entirety of the mediation fee. If the plaintiff does want this included as a condition of the deal, it should come out no later than the turning point.

On the other hand, the mediation fees can be an effective tool to use at the very last minute, to seal a deal or snap the last little gap closed. If counsel prefers, he may keep this tactic in his pocket until needed – with the understanding that if it is not needed as a tool or crowbar at the very end to pull the ends together, then counsel cannot pull it out of his pocket at the last minute and add it as an independent "Oh, by the way ..." additional condition.

The objective of the "empty all pockets" time is to avoid having any additional term or new condition come out at the very last minute, on the final move, as a surprise. Countless deals have been impaled forever upon the miss-timed list of additional considerations that come out too late.

Home plate

If it is going to work, eventually everyone in the ballpark will be standing around home plate.

The fact that it is "home plate" and not second base, or a pizza box bouncing along the right field fence, may not have been truly ascertained or ascertainable until all the parties actually reach the place and are standing around it. But once everybody is there, it cannot be missed. The final step is to stamp on it and declare the game over.

The turning point marks that move where the parties stop searching around the ballpark for home plate and actually begin to close in upon it. Sometimes you can tell when the dialogue transitions, sometimes it is seamless. There may be a change in the pace or the tempo of the moves, there may be a hitch – or not. Sometimes one must just assume that the turning point was reached. However on reaches this point, there are certain things that have to be attended to once the negotiation makes the turn and heads for the ending.

The almost universal closing in a market haggle comes when one or the other says, "OK, split the difference and we're done." The same is often true in litigation mediation, although a sizable number are resolved when the paying insurer declines to accept the invited midpoint exactly and makes an offer a few thousand short of that, declaring such to be the "last, best and final." Usually, this is pure power play, based upon the size and might of the insurance company writing the checks.

Where the parties are of equal stature, however, the dead-on split is very common.

The mistake that can be made now is for one party to decide to try and improve the deal. The negotiation has arrived at a figure within the acceptance value range of all sides. While all may be satisfied with the apparent answer, no one side is going to be truly happy; each side may well feel that their side has given up the greater part of the compromises, may feel stressed that they have stretched their expectations value this far, and may feel quite tired and burned out by the process. The only acceptable move, at this point, is a move to converge.

What may blow everything apart is for one party to decide that the deal is not quite good enough, and that with just a round or two more, it can be made perfect. So they change the objective – they try to move home plate – in the words of author Spencer Johnson, they "move the cheese." This kind of move is truly toxic and can blow the whole deal to smithereens.

The mediator will try to ensure that this doesn't happen. He will endeavor to ensure that by the end of the day, the only true option available to either party will be converging upon the now plainly visible objectives of home plate.

Once the acceptance values finally appear in the immediate range, and either at or very close to home plate, the only expected result from that point to the end are a fine-tuning move or two for adjustment, and then for someone to say, "OK, done."

It's not rocket science, and there are no secret, mystical talents involved. All that is needed to succeed is preparation, patience, persistence, and careful attention to detail.

18
Rescues and such

Unilateral declarations of value

Assume a situation where the dialogue has been unsuccessful in bringing parties to the ballpark.

One party is close within reach of its expectations, but the other party is still wandering around in the parking lot – or worse, appears to be headed back to for mountains where they started. Nobody seems to be paying attention to the normal dialogue.

The bidding party does not want to call off the settlement negotiations until the other side is fairly advised on what the offering party is prepared to do. What is needed is for the bidding party to indicate clearly where it believes the ending value to be, but the values are not close enough to use either a split or conditional offer. One technique is to state what the bidding party determines to be the final number and declare simply that it is the last, best and final offer, and then stop. The problem here is one of transparency and credibility; somebody has not been paying attention, and is not aware of how close to the end the dialogue really is. The problem with a sudden declaration now, without warning, is credibility and surprise. The other side may not believe the statement, and if they do, they will feel double-crossed because they will think it came without warning.

A better way to demonstrate a unilateral declaration of the ending value is to let the numbers speak by delivering the message within the negotiation dialogue in a planned set of moves.

There are two such methods, one with straight moves, the other using conditionals.

Convergent moves. This is used when the opponent is way off base in the values, and is substantially higher or lower than the bidder's intended target. The method: Take the distance between the offering bidder's present bid location and the target location and plan to span that distance in a set pattern of three or four moves, independent of any response from the opponent, with each move being approximately half value of the previous move. The pattern will describe a series of sharply decreasing values which, within two or three rounds, will unmistakably point at the target value. It is not possible for the opposing side to misunderstand the message.

For example, take a defendant at 20 chips and a plaintiff at 500 chips. The value the defendant is willing to accept and pay is 100 chips, but plaintiff is refusing to make any significant moves in that direction. The defendant plans moves to the target in 4 or 5 moves, starting with a move that is half the present distance to the target, and with each succeeding move being half the value of before. The moves from 20 in sequence are: add 40, add 20, add 10, add 5, add 2.5. In this sequence, the defendant does not care what the opponent's moves are.

If one is keeping track, the moves would go from 20 to 60, then 80, then 90, then 95 on the fourth move. Then, if necessary, 97.5 on the fifth move. The final move would be to 100, accompanied by the statement that this number is the last, best and final. This way, when the final offer is made, any transparency problem will have been resolved; the final demand will not come as a surprise, there is no double cross, and the sincerity of the offers can be ascertained by the consistency of the moves.

What is important here is that these moves are made independently of any moves by the other side. Whether the other side stays high around 500, or suddenly breaks and moves near 100 is not relevant; the strategy is to keep with the pattern moves to the end. If the plaintiff is still above 400 or so when you finally get to 100 and say last and final, that's it. He either can accept or everybody goes home. Of course, if he breaks and says how about 120, the defendant can decide. But if he was willing to drop from 400 or so to 120 in one move, surely he will accept 100. It becomes a test of wills.

The tougher call is when the plaintiff wakes up earlier. He sees the omen when the defense is about half way, and suddenly begins to drop on his own. When the defense has reached its penultimate 98, say, the plaintiff has smoothly dropped down to 122.

What's going on?

Plaintiff has positioned himself to start matching the defendant and offering a new middle at 110. Defense goes to 99, plaintiff goes to121. Defense goes to 100 and says all in, plaintiff goes to 120 and says he is all done. Now who is bluffing who? Neither one can try the case for 20 chips, so who is going to blink? It becomes a test of wills.

Convergent with Conditional Brackets. This technique is especially useful when it appears that the plaintiff has a midpoint in mind that he is trying to get the defendant to accept, and the defense wants one that is somewhat lower, but both sides are close and the offering bidder does not really want to jeopardize the entire effort.

For example, assume the parties are at 270 chips and 350 chips. Plaintiff is driving for 300, and the defense wants to settle at 290. Defendant offers to add a straight 10 chips to 280, with a conditional at 290. (Format of the conditional: "We move up 10 to 280 chips, but if you will offer to take 290, we will accept.") No matter what move plaintiff makes, the defense makes a pattern move as if in the previous pattern, with the straight move to 285, then a move to 287, and then 289, continuing to extend the conditional of 290 each time. Finally the last move matches the conditional at 290, when the bidder can declare this to be final. Using either of these methods gives up any chance of settling the case at a lower figure than selected by the defense for the target number, but is the best method of setting out the target and getting to it, or within an acceptable value near it, within the framework of the negotiation.

Crossing barriers

For some reason, very large round numbers encountered as the parties converge may seem to pose barriers to progress. For example, suppose the parties start out at 300 by plaintiff and 50 by defendant, with a predicted target of around 125. To make it sound worthwhile, assume the chips are worth $1000 each.

It is not unusual for there to be a hitch in the process as the plaintiff's number approaches the 200 level, and a correlative hitch as the defense offers reach the 100 level. The chips can be worth 1 or whatever power of 10 is needed. It is a curious phenomenon that does not seem to have any real basis, but does seem to happen now and then. When such potential barriers are encountered, the move will take one of three shapes. (1) The most productive is a non-hitched pattern move that is consistent with prior moves and crosses the barrier without a pause. (2) The least disruptive of the barrier moves is the move that is out of pattern but stops dead on the barrier. (3) The potentially dangerous hitch is where the party pulls up short of the barrier, and stays shy by a small amount. The parties were at 165 and 85 with defendant to move. The predicted move is a 20 move to 105 on the way to 125 but instead the defense offers 97.

The pull up short of the barrier makes the third move much more dangerous. The risk is that the defense has a little room to work with, and may make it into a true barrier here. If the plaintiff gives him something to work with by making a full move from 165 to 145, the next defense move may only be to 98, staying on the wrong side of the barrier and leaving the plaintiff with no good options. There is at least some danger of the whole process stalling out.

If the hitch is a move to the barrier dead on, i.e., 100 instead of 105, the best response is to simply mirror the move – down 15 to 150 – keeping the midpoint in the same place, and waiting to see if the defense moves off the barrier and back to the pattern without further ado on the next move.

If the hitch is shy of the barrier, however, a slightly more aggressive move is indicated. Say the plaintiff was planning on moving from 165 to 145 if the defense had gone to 105 as expected – now faces the pull-up of 97K. While a mirror of 12K down, matching the defense move may work just fine, a more aggressive move would be to put out a short move on the plaintiff side with a suggested bracket. Plaintiff moves only down 5 to 160, but says they will move to 145 if the defense moves to 105. In other words, the plaintiff pulls up even shorter than the defendant, but offers a bracket that will pull the defendant through the barrier and put both parties back where they would have been with a completed pattern move. If the defense plays any games, the plaintiff is better positioned with options.

A difficulty comes if the barrier is on the back end of the exchange instead of going in.

If the plaintiff had been the first to move in the last example, and had made the pattern move to 145, and then the defense makes the pull up to 97, the parties are now in a different position. The delta is 48 with 121 in the middle. Plaintiff has to move, but does not have a good pattern move available. Best here a short move plus a bracket, say a move to 140 but a bracket at 115 and 135. If the defense accepts, this would put the process back with the same number in the middle, but jumping it along faster. The real question is what is the defendant going to do – stay under 100 chips or break out? Defendant may draw the line under 100 or may break out and create his own new bracket, proposing a new midpoint. As long as plaintiff recognizes the need hold back and create options in the face of the pull-up, there will be the time and opportunity to test all the potential avenues. The thing is not going to turn into a trainwreck.

If all the barriers are successfully overcome and the parties finally cross the parking lot, get their hotdogs and move onto the outfield grass, the mediation is about to head into the final stages.

The mediator's solution

This is rarely seen any more, but was a popular device some years ago, and variations may surface from time to time. The parties get stuck at a distance apart where a settlement should result, but for some reasons, neither side is willing to move closer.

In the example used throughout the book, where the parties start at 1,000 and 0, the plaintiff is at 360 and the defense is at 335 and neither party is willing to budge. In the mediator's solution, the mediator writes a number on two pieces of paper, and gives one to each side. He asks both parties to caucus and then tell him yes or no whether they would accept the number he has written as the settlement number for the case. The number, usually close to the midpoint, is between the two values where the parties are stuck.

If both sides say yes, the case is settled at that figure. If only one says yes, there is no settlement, but the mediator does not tell anyone that somebody said yes. He just announces that the case did not settle. The party saying yes does not risk having the other side learn that they would have budged from their announced position.

Mediators do not like this method, for it injects the mediator into the substantive decision making. If the mediator picks a value and the case does not settle, eventually the mess turns into the mediator's fault because he picked the wrong number.

In most cases, experience has taught that if the parties are close enough that they should have settled at conference, a hiatus for a couple of days will usually soften the hard edges and permit the parties themselves to figure out an acceptable solution. Or the mediator, in follow up calls to the lawyers, can get the parties re-interested in trying, and work in a few bidding rounds by telephone or email to bridge the gap. The mediator does not have to get involved in being the one to select values for the final deal.

The final word

In market place negotiations, one has plenty of options if the deal goes south. Litigation negotiation, on the other hand, has only one alternative. The parties cannot choose to deal with someone else; they cannot change brands; and they cannot decide to shop later. If the parties to a litigation negotiation do not make a deal, their case is on the rails headed for a jury courtroom. And if that happens, they lose all control over the outcome.

Negotiation, whether direct or with the assistance of a mediator, allows the parties to retain control. In litigation situations, if the parties cannot come to acceptable terms to resolve the dispute, that does not mean the case won't settle. It is not a question of whether the case will settle, it is a matter of who is going to do it.

After a failed negotiation by the parties, the decision will be made by a group of total strangers with no interest in the case, no stake in the outcome, and no technical expertise over any part of it. This group will be given only a limited amount of time to learn the facts, and, if they are asked the question and permitted to answer, they will all say they would be rather be doing something else.

Does this sound like a description of a jury trial? The jury trial is a Constitutional right, the bedrock of our judicial system, and ingrained in our history and culture. We have the best system in the world, and there is nothing wrong with taking a case into court. There is no question that the jury trial is a valuable resource.

Nevertheless, through effective negotiation, and especially with the guidance of a skilled mediator, the parties themselves, who have the most at stake in the outcome and have the most knowledge of all material circumstances, can maintain control in a process that will always accommodate the most flexible solutions possible.

The jury trial is a fine part of our system, but from every logical and legal viewpoint, settlements are better.

A Mediator's dream

Author's note: What follows is completely made up – it's total fiction. But it actually happened. Every word was spoken by a real lawyer to the author as a mediator in a real case. The pieces and parts are real; the whole is not. The object is to illustrate what this book is all about.

(On the letterhead of retired judge Martin Mediator, who is in a private practice limited to Alternative Dispute Resolution services, which includes general civil case mediation.)

J. Gordon Gettem, Jr. Esq.
Dewey Gettem & Howe
Midwest Bank Building, 2d Floor
410 West Main Street
Capital City, Anystate

Naomi K. Alloway, Esq.
Alloway Autta Town & Beck
Central Bank Plaza, Suite 1100
101 East Main Street
Capital City, Anystate

Re: Peter Pulling v Diana Dearhart

Dear Counsel:

This confirms your engagement of me to mediate a settlement conference for the captioned matter on:

A date to be determined
Beginning at 9:30 a.m.

In conference facilities at the offices of Alloway Autta Town & Beck
3100 Bank Plaza, Suite 3100
Capital City

You are engaging me at my standard hourly fee, to be billed to counsel upon conclusion of the conference. My invoices will be to counsel, and are due from counsel upon receipt. I am not extending credit to clients. I understand that my fee is to be divided two ways, evenly between or among the lawyers to whom this letter is addressed.

You have identified all parties and counsel. I am acquainted with the lawyers and their firms. My acquaintance is professional, from appearances in my court, from unrelated ADR assignments, and from bar association activities which I do not consider to be a conflict under the circumstances of this case. I am not acquainted and/or have no connection with any of the parties. I am unaware of any circumstance that would prevent me from acting as the conference mediator in this case.

A settlement conference is subject to agreement of the parties, and you may modify any of these terms. Unless modified by specific agreement among counsel, with advice to me of the modification, and to ensure that there is no misunderstanding with regard to the settlement conference, here is what all parties have the right to expect.

All parties in interest and their lead counsel will attend the conference and participate in person. The representative at conference for a business or government entity will be an executive decision maker of the entity, who will be fully familiar with the file and who will have full and sufficient personal authority to authorize settlement of the case. It is not sufficient if the representative at conference is only a messenger or delegate who must report to and seek instructions from someone else.

Everyone has the right to expect that all participants will set aside the entire day, and into the evening hours if necessary, for this effort. I strongly recommend that participants traveling from afar not plan return travel accommodations until the next day.

If time must be constrained, all counsel – and me – should be notified in advance of the conference. I do recommend that consideration should first be given to rescheduling the conference. It is an unfair practice to announce after the conference has begun that time is limited because a participant intends to leave early.

If more than one person is required to make a decision for a party, then all who must agree should attend the conference and participate in person. If a number of individuals are involved, and all cannot attend the conference, those that do not attend will delegate full authority to settle to either their attorney or to others in the party who will be present. The delegation of authority should be in writing and revealed to the mediator and all other parties.

If a party defendant is fully insured, and the claim is within the limits of the insurance in force, the party is welcome at the conference but does not need to attend; it will be sufficient if the insurance carrier is represented as provided herein. If the claim exceeds the insurance in force, or if the insurer is defending under reservation of rights, the party should attend. If the party does not attend, and the plaintiff elects to proceed, it will be assumed that a settlement within insurance limits will resolve the case.

If a party defendant's consent is required for settlement, the party must attend, or must release the condition requiring consent in writing.

It is not sufficient for a representative to participate only by telephone unless all counsel agree in advance of the conference, with notice to me of their agreement.

I recommend that all counsel prepare a position paper for submission in advance of the conference, and share copies with all other counsel.

I have no particular format for a general position paper. What I am looking for is at least a skeleton outline or bullet point summary of the essential facts and legal theories. The extent of detail depends on the nature of the dispute. Circumstances that are disputed may require more detail to frame the circumstances that are not in dispute.

I do not require or recommend the disclosure of any strategic or tactical material in any paper shared with the opposition, such as strengths and weaknesses, counsel's estimates of settlement potential or counsel's estimates of settlement ranges. (These topics will be covered in private caucus with each side at the conference.)

If any party intends to submit a position paper to me but does not intend to share it with the opposition, counsel should so notify opposing counsel.

Whether position papers are exchanged or not, any parties claiming damages should provide a detailed itemization of all special damages claimed, together with appropriate foundation for the claims, to all other parties prior to the conference. It is usually a huge waste of time for counsel to be presented with the specifics of special damage claims for the first time at a settlement conference.

Unless the materials are voluminous, it is sufficient if I receive anything submitted one day before the conference. (For voluminous materials, advance the submission date to me by a sufficient time to give me a chance to read and study what I need to know before the day of the conference.)

Papers may be mailed, emailed or faxed to any of the addresses indicated on this letterhead. For hand or courier delivery, please contact me for my street address as I do not publish it or release it unless there is a need to know.

I do not make any report to the court unless there is a court order and I am requested to do so by counsel. If you wish me to make a report to the court, please provide me with a copy of the court order. My report, if any, will be only the information required by rule.

I consider all details of a settlement conference to be confidential EXCEPT (1) the name of the case, (2) the identity of the lawyers, (3) the subject matter of the dispute, and (4) the fact of whether the case settled at conference.

After the conference, I will discard (or return, if requested) all position papers and other materials submitted. I do not retain my notes. I keep only electronic data consisting of administrative correspondence and billing information.

Unless you advise me of other considerations, I assume that the provisions of this letter, together with the provisions of the relevant rules of civil procedure and local court rules, will be sufficient for the protection of all parties, and that no further written agreement, either between the parties or with me, is required.

Unless you advise me otherwise, I assume that I may contact any counsel separately upon any matter pertaining to the conference, either before or after the conference.

My invoices will be to counsel, and are due from counsel upon receipt. I am not extending credit to clients. If anyone wishes different arrangements, contact me before the conference.

Finally, I am being retained to mediate a settlement conference and not to adjudicate any issue. I am not and will not act as counsel to any party. My approach is proactive and directive, but I stress at all times that any decision to settle rests exclusively with the parties and their counsel, and not me.

Your acceptance of this letter, both on your behalf and as counsel for the parties you represent, constitutes our agreement. If there are other matters to be addressed, please let me know.

Sincerely,

Martin Mediator

Note: The mediator's letter contains all the details that would be expected to convene a mediation. Some mediators use formal contracts, with all parties signing. Others use the engagement letter approach. It is important the mediation arrangement be in writing.

(On the letterhead of J. Gordon Gettem, Jr., attorney at law.)

Hon. Martin Mediator
1100 Justice Drive
Capital City, Anystate

Re: Peter Pulling v Diana Dearhart

Dear Judge Mediator:

Thank you for agreeing to mediate the caption matter for us. Please accept this letter as our mediation statement.

The facts are straight forward. Ms. Dearhart was operating her car at a high rate of speed and blew through the stop sign at 12th and Main. Mr. Pulling was approaching the intersection from Ms. Dearborn's right. He had the right of way both because of the stop sign and because he was on her right. He did not have time to avoid the accident. His vehicle, a late model Honda SUV, was struck on the left rear quarter panel, spinning it around and flipping it over. Mr. Pulling was not wearing his seatbelt, and was ejected from the vehicle. He sustained multiple contusions and abrasions, a concussion, a fracture of the clavicle, multiple fractures of the left arm requiring surgical reduction, deep lacerations and fractures of the left leg, and multiple fractures of his left foot requiring surgical reduction.

Mr. Pulling is a CPA, and was incapacitated for about six weeks during tax season. After six weeks, he was able to return to work in a wheel chair, and gradually improved. He has fully recovered from his injuries with the exception of the multiple fractures to his left arm. He is left with a severely damaged left arm, with range of motion reduced by 60%, and strength reduced by 80%. This does not affect his work, but severely interferes with his previous recreational activities, which include skiing, golf, outdoor activities with his son, and playing the piano. The damage to his left arm is considered permanent.

Mr. Pulling's specials, which we understand are not disputed, consist of $67,525 in medical expenses, much of which relate to the surgeries required for his arm and foot; $15,000 lost income, being $2,500 per week for the six weeks he was incapacitated, for a total of $82,525.

Ms. Alloway and I have discussed the possibility of settlement, but no offers have been exchanged. We look forward to working with you next week.

Sincerely,

J. Gordon Gettem, Jr.

c: Naomi Alloway

(On the letterhead of Naomi Alloway, attorney at law.)

Hon. Martin Mediator
1100 Justice Drive
Capital City, Anystate

Re: Pulling v Dearhart

Dear Martin:

I join Gordon in thanking you for agreeing to help us here. I agree generally with Gordon's recitation of fact, with the following additions:

Our client did blow the stop sign. I am not sure what Gordon meant by the reference to a high rate of speed. The accident reconstruction report indicates that the Dearborn vehicle was proceeding at about 30 mph into the intersection, which would have been the speed limit, but for the stop sign. The Pulling vehicle, however, was proceeding in excess of 40 mph in a 35 mph zone. We believe there will be some component of comparative negligence assigned to Mr. Pulling on account of this speed.

We agree with the recitation of injuries, the recuperation, and Mr. Pulling's present status. As to medical specials, we agree that the figure stated was what was invoiced; however, the medicals were covered by Mr. Pulling's Blue Cross coverage, which had contracts with all the providers. The actual payment by the medical insurer after the contractual adjustments was considerably less than the amount invoiced.

On Mr. Pulling's claim for lost income, we would note that he did have his computer at the hospital and at home. During this period of his incapacitation, he invoiced just over $8,000 in client billings, which we understand were paid.

We do not dispute the permanent damage to Mr. Pulling's left arm. We would note that he was very seldom on the golf course before the accident, having played only five times in the last three years. He was an avid skier, and since the accident he has joined his son in snow-boarding. You don't use poles in snowboarding, and the left arm damage is not a hindrance. As to his piano playing, he only started lessons a year and a half ago. And was still at level one when the accident occurred.

No offers have been made prior to the conference. We will see you next week.

Yours truly,

Naomi Alloway

c: Gordon Gettem

Preliminary session

Everyone appeared at the appointed time. The judge made sure everyone knew everyone else, then introduced himself and explained the how the mediation would work. He had worked with both lawyers often, and he knew that they had explained all this to their clients. He covered quickly how the caucuses would work, what his role was, and what the parties might expect. He stressed that he was not there to be a judge, but just to help the parties and the lawyers in the negotiation.

"Mediation is guided negotiation," the judge told everybody, "I am here to be a guide, a coach, an instructor, a message carrier, all about the process of negotiation. I am not here to be a judge. I am going to stay out of the lawyers' way on issues of substance. I know enough about trials to know where problems might crop up, but I don't know enough about your case to know whether these problems are case-swallowing ogres or minor speed bumps. I leave quantifying the problems to the lawyers. I run process, and that means I am the one to say that it isn't working. I promise not to waste your time. If this isn't working, we will stop. But we are not going to stop until I have made sure that the impasse is for real, and we cannot figure a way around it."

The mediator quickly went over the matter of confidentiality, what would be reported to the court, if anything, and the necessity for a written agreement if the case did settle. Then he finished with, "Any questions? None? OK, Gordon, you are the plaintiff so I am going to start with you. Naomi says you are in the conference room just down the hall. Let's split up now and get started." The mediator zipped up his case and followed Gordon Gettem and his client out the door.

The mediator was a retired state court trial judge who regularly conducts civil case mediations. He sat at the table with the plaintiff and his counsel for their first private caucus in the case. The lawyer, Gordon Gettem, was a seasoned plaintiff's lawyer with over 25 years' experience. He estimated the value of the case to be a strong argument in plaintiff's favor, but with some risk because his client had been speeding just before the accident. Gettem categorized it as a somewhat iffy case with a 70-30 odds factor in plaintiff's favor. He had read the mediator's book and had very roughly calculated a normal verdict. While he originally started out with $74,000 in fixed specials, he was reducing his claim for specials to $44,000 to reflect an adjustment for the amount the health carrier actually paid the providers under their HMO contracts, and eliminating the $8,000 lost earnings while his client was recuperating. His estimate of the general damage component, based upon his client's injuries, was $300,000 for a mid-range verdict, making a combined valuation of $344,000.

Applying his probability estimate of 70% resulted in an adjusted probable total verdict of $240,000. The best day aspirations value was around $390,000, his tentative estimated acceptance value to be around $190,000 to $205,000.

Now, at mediation, the opening session and greetings are out of the way, and the parties are headed into the first private caucus session with the mediator to plan and deliver the first round moves. The plaintiff's side goes first, and the task at hand was to decide on the first round demand to send over to the defense side. No formal discussion of settlement had occurred in the case.

Round 1

As soon as everyone was settled at the table, the mediator asked the first question to plaintiff's counsel. "What do you want to do here, Gordon, start by making an anchoring move, or pass the wand over to the defense?"

"What are the considerations we should be looking at here?" the lawyer asked, hoping to get the mediator's insight into the strategy that should be employed here.

"Your first move strategy depends upon on how strongly you feel about your chances of winning here," the judge began to explain. "If it is actually an iffy case, with some chance of a zero lurking out there, the ultimate control is probably going to be with the defense – the result is going to be a compromise, and what you need to know is how much are they putting on their chance of winning, and how much are they willing to spend before they tip the table over and insist on a trial. At this point, only the defense knows how they have calculated the odds and what values they put on the various parts, so the knowledge edge at this point is with them.

"On the other hand, if the case is actually a certain winner from a liability standpoint, with little or no chance of a defense verdict, and where the only issue is really going to be how much is the probable verdict going to be, then what the defense is very interested in is what you think a jury might bring in, and how much will you discount this thing off that expected jury result in order to get it done today? On this side, the knowledge edge at this point is with you – what is your evaluation of a probable verdict, what kind of discount can be engineered to get the case resolved now, and what your appetite is for taking this into a jury courtroom."

"What difference does this make in the decision on making the opening move?" Gordon asked.

"In the long run, probably not any difference," the judge replied. "The negotiation dialogue will eventually settle into a pattern that will indicate where all these questions will be answered. Typically, the side with the knowledge edge will eventually control the pace and velocity of the negotiation. It may remain with the same side throughout, it may get passed back and forth. At this point, if you think you have the knowledge edge and you want to show it, then your objective might be to begin a dialogue that will tell opposition from the outset where they have to be in order to settle the case. On the other hand, if you think they might have the knowledge edge at this point, you may not want to tip your hand at all until you find out more about their side. You may want them to lead with you making the decision at each turn on how best to follow. This thing isn't going to settle without your consent, and the opening move is not going to sell the farm, so don't worry. The difference here is only in the nuances."

"Okay, I get that. Now, how do we do all those things in an opening bid or a single number?" he asked.

"The opening bidder in a negotiation has three options here: make what we call a "random move" which means put up a number that says nothing about anything, it just passes the move over to the other side. Or you can make a "relevant" move, which says you are interested, you're here to deal, but provides no further information. It simply conveys that you want the other side to go first. Finally, you can make what is called an "anchor" move which can pile on a whole bunch of information. It demonstrates that you are not only interested but connected to this process and sensitive to the ranges of the other side, and it will convey to a receiver who is paying attention an obvious indication of where you believe the center or target area of the mediation to be. Believe it or not, you can do all these things with a single number."

The judge turned to a whiteboard and picked up a marker. "In this case, you told me when we talked on the phone about this that your aspirations value to be $390,000." As he spoke, he wrote the figure on the whiteboard. "A random move would be a move above your aspirations figure that did not give any clue yet as to what the aspiration or any other value might be. It can be way up the clouds or just a little cut above, doesn't matter. The difference between your aspiration and expectation value is $150,000, and this delta is usually a good measure to add to the aspirations to get into the random territory with a first move – so here, adding

$150,000 to the aspirations value means anything around or above $530,000 would be a random move." He wrote the figures on the whiteboard too, then continued, "The sole purpose of the random move is to pass the baton to the other side without indicating anything about your case. But it is usually not a progressive idea to make the random move too high. The move should be above where you expect a jury might go – you do not intend that the opening demand be accepted – but you do not want it laughed at."

"Now, to make a relevant move, you need it to be relevant to your side of the case – maybe within reach of your aspirations value. At or above it, but not too far above it. You might even be a little bit below it, but not too far below. It needs to be a number that might conceivably by something the jury could award. The idea is to indicate that you are serious about the effort and are here to give this matter your full interest and attention, but not necessarily your commitment to the process until the other side speaks. The primary purpose of a relevant move is to pass the baton to the other side, but it is to also demonstrate that you are paying attention and you are interested in pursuing settlement."

The plaintiff's lawyer said, "I think I want to find out where Naomi is coming from before I turn over all my cards, so I think we want to use either a random or relevant move here for the first go. What would you think of starting at $500,000 or maybe $750,000 to begin with?"

The judge said, "You told me that prior to the mediation, you had already suggested a handful of times the value of $480,000 and got no response. So, if you assume that Naomi was paying attention, and even though these comments of yours were not formal demands, wouldn't any starting number above $480,000 number be suggesting a range above one that has already been hinted at and declined? One of the labels of a random move is that it is, or it points at a number that is probably outside the acceptable range of bidding, but not something that has already been turned down. If you make it too far outside, you might send the wrong signal. And it is always a difficult signal to appear to be moving backwards. So even $500,000 here would be just over the edge – you would be moving backwards from what you suggested before the mediation. It might not do any damage to the message because it is just a little bit too high, but starting high 'just because' could be a lot worse. Not terrible, horrible, awful worse, because it is not illegal or against the rules to make a random move at a very high number, or even one that goes backwards from an offer made before the mediation but that wasn't accepted. But it just might slow things down while the opposition works and fusses until you bring your numbers back to at least something below where you were before we started."

"What if we start at $480,000 – the figure I kept mentioning? What does that say?"

"Dead on the bubble – right on the fence. More random than relevant, but it does have some indicia of a relevant move since it does connect to what was said before. Certainly not an aggressive or progressive move, since it does not advance the ball any, but probably does no harm because you are not going backwards. And it moves the turn to the other side."

"Okay," said Gordon, "What about an opening move just a little under $480,000? If I take the aspirations of $390,000 and split that difference I get $435,000. What would that say?"

"With your pre-mediation discussions with Naomi, that bid now becomes a relevant move," the mediator explained. "In one number, it carries several positive messages – that you are aware of the conversations that have gone on up to this time, and by using your special damage figure you are connected to the values that were expressed before, and you are interested in seeing where this will go. And the little tiny move off the bubble says you are going to be very cautious. All that can be extracted from that one number – and frankly, if anyone has any trouble interpreting those messages, I will be right there to help them read the signals. It's right on the edge of where you were before the mediation, but where something above the $480,000 number would be a random move since it is clearly too high, the 435 figure is inside the range – you are under every number you might have mentioned before the mediation, and this indicates a willingness negotiate which is positive, and shows both an awareness and interest in the process, but you are still a good ways away from even your most optimistic value. This is the definition of a relevant move. Just a few thousand moves the bid from random to relevant."

"Let's do it this way. Naomi is complaining that my specials are too high because of some lost earnings claim while Peter was recuperating and the health insurer's contract adjustments off the invoiced medicals. The total she is complaining is $32,475. If I take that away from the $480,000, I get $447,525. What if we start there"

"Good as any, plus I can explain your adjustment and ensure that they see it as a try at a relevant adjustment," the judge said.

"Also, it will take that complaint off the table for good. That sounds like what we want to do here," said Gordon. If my client agrees, I recommend that we start with an opening demand of $447,525." The client was nodding his agreement.

The mediator jotted the numbers onto his pad, zipped up his case and headed out the door to the defense side to deliver the opening salvo.

Round 1 continued

Naomi Alloway and the claims manager of Northwest Mutual were in a separate conference room just down the hall from Gordon Gettem and the plaintiff. The defendant, Diana Dearborn, was not present. Since she was fully insured for any loss that might arise, her presence was not needed at the mediation, and she had no interest in attending.

After getting himself a fresh cup of coffee, the judge sat down and, without unzipping his case yet, asked Naomi what her take on the case was.

"We think it's probably one of your iffy cases, from your iffy-bad quadrant. It's an intersection case with a very bad result, and we did blow the stop sign and it was our fault. But Pulling was driving too fast, and it very well could become his case to lose. If he does something dumb, or Gordon irritates the jury in some way, or we catch lightening in the bottle, there is at least a chance that that the jury will come on the issue of comparative negligence at 50 – 50 and this thing goes south. We are not banking on anything like that happening, and we are here to settle this case if Gordon will be reasonable. We put the risk factor in the 60-40 or maybe 65-35 range."

"Or 70% on your client and 30% on the plaintiff? He was only going about 3 miles over the speed limit, wasn't he? Who do you expect the jury to identify with here?" the mediator inquired, with an eyebrow raised.

"We are not putting too much on the comparative, Martin, we can see that. But we are going to get a jury instruction and blanks on the verdict form for the jury to fill in on the issue of comparative, and it is a risk. Strange things can happen at trial. You know that." Naomi defended her position.

"Who's your judge?" the mediator asked.

Naomi named one of the newer judges, recently appointed. "We don't know much about her. She came up through the prosecutor's route and we don't think she has had too much civil trial experience. We are not putting a factor in for the judge, one way or the other."

"Well, from what you tell me, you and Gordon are looking at this case about the same way from a risk standpoint. Of course, you see the glass as half empty and he sees it as half full, but that is natural and will factor itself into the process once we get something going. Gordon says there wasn't much in the way of settlement discussions before this mediation – you agree?"

"He's right. I floated a trial balloon or two, but Gordon came back with numbers so high it didn't make any sense to open up anything before the mediation. So, no, there has not been any serious discussion of settlement up to now."

"Well, let's get started then." The judge unzipped his case. "Gordon starts with $447,525 for full release and settlement of all claims and dismissal of all litigation. He wants you to now that that number includes the specials reduced by $32,475, which are the items you complained to him about."

"Oh, for God's sake. Martin, he's got his head in the clouds. The number he was bandying about before we got into this was $480,000, and that subtraction was bogus. Those items never should have been in there and he knows it, he is not giving up a thing there. I told him then he was way, way too high. We have no intention of playing any games here, and we won't respond until he makes a realistic offer that we can work with."

Naomi pretended to be highly offended, but the mediator had been in enough of these to know that it was largely an act. She might have been hoping for a lower starting number, but the number given was not a complete surprise, and she knew it, and she knew the mediator knew it.

"Well, let's take a look at this. What was the trial balloon that you popped up with prior to this?

"It was just a suggestion, it was not a true offer," Naomi said.

"I understand Gordon thought it was pretty low. Would the $480,000 be in response to your number being too low, or did you think it was an independent opening demand by the plaintiff?" the mediator replied.

"No, no – these were just suggestions, testing the water. There were no actual offers exchanged," she said.

"Did you ever suggest that you would offer any more than what your trial balloon suggested?" the judge asked.

"No, it never got that far."

"How many times did you bring up your number?" he said.

"Twice. Maybe three times. What are you getting at here?" Naomi asked.

"Take a look at this from Gordon's side. You said you mentioned two or three times that you would be interested in settling the case and suggested the same lowball number each time. Each time, Gordon showed no interest at your number and put out a much higher number. But you did not come off your number. Right?" The judge got himself a fresh cup of coffee.

"Well, yeah, But these weren't hard offers."

"And now Gordon has made a hard offer at $447,525. Which is considerably below what he was floating earlier. What does that say?" the judge asked.

"That he is still too high. He was at $480,000 and we told him it was too high and that he had to come down," she said.

"And he did, right?"

"But not enough. Tell him we will respond when he makes a rational demand." Naomi said.

"No, that's not how it works. You don't get to grade his response and start demanding do-overs. Negotiation is a dialogue, and if it is going to work, it has to constantly move forward. Making him select another number would be making him bid against himself, which is not productive. The only exception to that is if the bid was his final bid, and you wanted to decline. But his number is not a final bid, it is the first bid in what is supposed to be a dialogue. He has made an opening demand, he has moved off where he might have been earlier, and this move deserves a response. You can tell him in the response – in the number you choose to send back – how you feel about his number."

"What are my options here?" Naomi asked.

"You are making the first bid, so you have a number of options. First, you can just put something out there. Pick your own opening bid, without regard to what he offered. You will clarify your position with the next round. You have the same options here as any opening bidder, to make a random or relevant or anchor bid. We've talked about all these before, so you know what I am talking about. Or you can treat his opening bid as part of the dialogue started before – he bid $480,000 , you said a number, he says $447,525 and it's your move – "

"No, no, that's not how it went," Naomi interrupted. "If he had said $480,000 first, I never would have come back with our number. It would have been far lower. If he is going to start around $480,000 we cannot be above 100,000. In fact, we have to be way under.

"OK, so what now, then?" the judge asked.

Naomi had not shared her analysis with the mediator, and he has not asked her to. Naomi estimated that the maximum verdict that might be sustained from this kind of case would be in the $360,000 range but that would be a home run with zero on the comparative negligence issue. She thinks that a more practical "best day" result would be around $240,000 to $260,000, and these would be impacted by the comparative negligence. Naomi thought that around 25% was within the expected range for the jury to find as comparative negligence on the plaintiff's part, making the final practical verdicts in the $175,000 – $180,000 range, taking the numbers off the $240,000 figure.

With all these considerations, in mind, Naomi and the claims manager had agreed that an acceptable settlement range for this case would be between $150,000 and $200,000. In her own mind, Naomi had pinned the maximum number at $180,000, but she did not know exactly where the claims manager for the insurance company would go.

"Alright, Judge, you talked us into staying." Naomi wrote a number on a slip of paper and showed it to the claims manager. He nodded. "Tell Gordon our response to his blue sky, cloud filled demand is $45,000."

"Pretty stiff, if Gordon thinks you were way above that."

"We have to drive that number out of his mind, if he is going up there over $400,000. You can tell him I can get to $140,000 and maybe above, but he has to come a long way off of $447,000. He is not warming my heart. Not yet."

Alright," said the judge, writing some notes onto his pad. He zipped up his case and started out. "Don't go far now."

Round 2

As the judge entered the conference room where Gordon Gettem and his client were waiting, he unzipped his case and pulled out his pad. The lawyer closed his laptop to give full attention to the judge.

"Opening move from the defense," he said, "is $45,000."

"What?" the lawyer exclaimed. "That is an insult, Judge, and you know it. They were at $100 thousand-something before the mediation, and they're going backwards. Well, we know what to do. Our move is to $480,000. Should have started there anyway."

"O.K. Gordon. Now take it easy. You made it clear that those preliminary numbers were not offers, right?" the judge said.

"Well, yeah, but $45,000 is absurd."

"Naomi does not expect you to accept it. It just an opening."

"Well, what do you recommend?" Gordon asked.

"You have to decide, but here are your options. First, you can either respond to her move or make an independent move. If you make an independent move, you have three options. You don't have rate of movement or delta to measure from the other side, but you can take your own. I guess you could say that the delta is from 0 to their opening move of $45,000, but that is really not supported. You can match your last move, make a bigger move or make a lesser move. A match is neutral – doesn't really convey that you are responding to anything from the other room, it just acknowledges that a move is needed. A larger move responds to the other side, and recognizes that you have to move closer to the target area before you are going to see anything significant from Naomi, and a smaller move says she has to show you something first, before you make any significant moves," the judge explained.

Gordon turned to his client and asked. "What do you think?"

"Let me make a recommendation here," the judge interrupted. "These early rounds are purely tactical signals. These are not real dollars on the table, they are just poker chips. Right now, there is nothing backing them up but the message. If this process is going to work, they will turn into real dollars eventually, but they are not there yet. Naomi doesn't expect you to accept what she is offering, and you did not seriously expect her to accept your demand. I strongly recommend to both sides that for these initial rounds, the lawyer drives the train. You make the decisions on the appropriate moves to get things into the ballpark. Once, or if and when, the numbers get into the ballpark, then, clearly, your client needs to participate and agree with what you are doing. But until then, this is all legal mumbo-jumbo, it's just strategy and tactics in the process of looking for the ballpark."

"I understand," Gordon said, and turned again to his client. "Are you O.K with that?" The client nodded his agreement.

"Then here's what I want to do. I will make a major drop, down to $397,525. That's a move of $50,000, and we need to see a major move from the defense."

"Very good, let's see what happens," said the judge, as he started out the door towards the other conference room.

Round 2 continued

The second conference room was just down the hall, and it took only few seconds for the judge to make his way to the door. He gave the door a sharp tattoo as he entered to get their attention.

"Plaintiff dropped from $447,525 to $397,525," he announced as he settled into his chair.

"Huh." Naomi did not seem happy. "O.K, we'll go to $50,000."

"Up 5? What do you want to do, end this before lunch? I had a hard enough time keeping him in the room when he though you went backwards last time. Now you come up $5000 on a $50,000 move. What message do you want to send?"

"That he is still way too high."

"And you are still way too low. So what do you want him to do, just guess at where he needs to be?"

"Well, what do you think we ought to do?" Naomi shot back.

"It has to be your decision, but look – where does his offer come from, can you tell?"

"Sure." Naomi scribbled some numbers on her pad. "It's his special damages, fully loaded plus $315,000. Look," she said, "a $315,000 verdict would be a great verdict all by itself on those damages, but he is not even there. First, his specials damages are too high. The medical invoices are not the right amount, it's the actual insurance payments, which were a lot less. We are still trying to pull it together, but we think it will be around $40,000, not $67,000. Second, his guy was working from his bed at the hospital and billing clients long before the six weeks were up. We know of at least $8,000 he billed from the hospital and we have no idea yet what he billed from home. I'll bet the specials don't add up to more than $50,000 when we get all the numbers in. And that's going to impact the general damages. And on top of all that, he is going to get hit for comparative. I am going argue like hell for 50/50, and I just might get it if Gordon lets the greed monster in the room on his side. But no matter what, he's got to take a healthy amount off for comparative."

"He says he has already adjusted his bid by $32,475 to account for the special damage problem."

"Well, he is still way too high," the lawyer said.

"What if you give him a ratio move? He moved $50,000, you move up some ratio of that which, if continued, would put you in good range in, say five moves?" the judge suggested.

Naomi pulled her pad over to her again. "What if I go up $20,000 and he keeps coming down $50,000. In five moves he comes down $250,000 to $147,525 and we would go up $100,000 to $145,000. That works." Naomi writes some more figures on her pad. "If I went up $25,000 for each $50,000 he comes down, in four moves we would be at $145,000 and he would be at $197,525. We can work with that, too. Bud," she looked over at her client representative, "do you want to go along with a move of $25,000? That would put us at $70,000."

The insurance guy nodded.

"OK Judge," Naomi said. "We move to $70,000. And you are authorized to explain exactly how we got there, and why, in trying to get Gordon to come to his senses."

The judge wrote the numbers in his pad, zipped up the case and headed to the door. "You might as well order lunch for us all," he said, "we're going to be here a while."

Note: The earlier moves here were "relevant" and not "random," but did not reveal anything of the lawyer's interpretation of the case. This move is a ratio move, designed to place the parties in a realistic position in a few rounds. The message may not be apparent to the plaintiff's counsel yet, but this is the definition of an "anchor move" – its meaning will be clarified in the next few rounds. The anchor move does not have to be in one move, although it usually is. It can be an anchor series, demonstrating the full impact over several moves.

Round 3

The judge settled at the table with a fresh cup of coffee. "They moved up $25,000 to $70,000," he said.

"Not as much as I had hoped, but at least it's a start," said the lawyer, "Naomi have any messages for me?"

"She told me I could tell you everything," the judge said, "but that would take too long. Let me digest it for you. I think she understands that you think you have already adjusted the special damages, but she still thinks you are too high. So, she calculated that since you went down by $50,000, she would go up by $25,000. What do you think that's telling you?" the judge asked.

"I don't know, it's too early to tell. She is still way too low." Gordon said.

"Well, where do you think she is headed?" the judge asked.

"Let's see, if I move $50,000 and she moves $25,000, after four rounds we would be only about $50,000 apart – we would be someplace in the vicinity of $200,000 and they would be around $150,000. But that's too low." Gettem said.

"But what's the middle at that point?" the judge pressed.

"Hm. About 175, I guess."

"What did you tell me your target figure was?" the judge asked.

"It was $190,000, but that was supposed to be rock bottom," Gettem said.

"What do you want to do?" the judge asked.

"What if we make it $350,000? It's not quite a drop of $50,000 but pretty close, and it gets rid of the label of special damages," the lawyer said.

"Yes, and it gets rid of the rational base you have been clinging to. It is absolutely true that true progress usually cannot be made until both parties divorce themselves from whatever rational basis they felt was anchoring their numbers, and recognize that the final number is just going to be a figure out in the middle somewhere that has a rational basis in the negotiation but not a connection to the values either party thought inviolate at the beginning. So, letting go of those specific dollars is a good thing," the judge said.

Gettem turned to his client. "Any problem here?" he asked.

"Not yet," the client responded. "Let's see what happens."

The judge zipped up his case.

Round 3 continued

The judge caught Naomi walking back to her conference room from her office. "Gordon dropped almost $50,000. He dropped to $350,000 even, dropping $47,524." The judge said.

"Alright! I see a glimmer of hope here," Naomi said. "If we keep the same pattern, we would move exactly half of their $47,525, or $23,762.50."

"And I have a recommendation. If you want to split this move closely, round it up slightly to $24,000. Or be stingy and round it down to $23,000.The point is that Gordon dropped the specificity relating to the special damages with his move, which is a good sign. We've talked about this before. It is very progressive when the parties abandon any attachment they might have to specific values derived from their operations, and recognize that the case will settle for a compromise number selected from each of the parties' positions – meaning essentially a round number. Even though your specific number is related to the bidding, it would send a better signal if you show detachment from specific values, too."

"I agree," Naomi said, "let's go with the rounded $24,000 figure and see what happens. We raise our offer by $24,000 to $94,000.

Round 4

"Here's the move," the judge said as he entered the conference room, "$94,000. Up $24.000."

"Hah! Not bad, right on predictions. Why did she only move 24 instead of 25?" said the lawyer.

"Actually, it was intended as a match in whole numbers of half of your last move of $47,524," the judge explained.

"Well, were are at $350,000, do we just drop down to $300,000? Keep up the momentum?" Gettem asked.

"Nothing wrong with that strategy. But observe: Naomi is at $94,000, which is $6,000 off a $100,000 dollar boundary. Boundaries tend to hang people up, and here is no different. You might consider staying a little above the $300,000 boundary, just in case. So you don't get maneuvered at the last minute," the judge suggested.

"Would I go to $306,000? That puts me in exactly the same place above my barrier that she is below hers," Gettem said.

"And that is a great neutral move," said the mediator. "But you do have a chance to send a progressive move and still stay safe. Move closer than $6,000, which makes it a stronger move, but still leave yourself some room above the boundary, just in case," the judge said.

"What if I move to $302,000? Gives me a little bit of room just in case."

"That's a good move and accomplishes all the necessary objectives," the judge said. "Shall I take it back?"

"Yep," Gordon said, "Let's rumble."

Round 4 continued

"You are at $94,000. The claimant moved to $302,000," the judge announced as he walked into the room.

"That's an odd move. Oh, I see. He's set this up so he is some distance from the 300,000 line in case I get froggy about crossing the 100,000 line. Martin, you should never have written that book. Everybody is spooked about barriers. Shall I give him something to think about and move to $98,000 or $99,000?" Naomi asked.

"Well, it's your call."

"How about we try a conditional. I make a formal move to $95,000 but I will move to $125,000 if he moves to $225,000 – the intent is to put $175 in the middle." Naomi said.

"Might this be too early the show your hand?" the judge asked.

"Maybe, but if I stay on this side of $100,000 to make the move as a conditional, I have a lots of protection. You are right about the big numbers being barriers and slowing things down. Here's our move: $95,000 firm, but we'll go to $125,000 if they move to $225,000."

"Stand by." The mediator zipped up his case and headed for the door.

Round 5

"OK, the formal move is from $94,000 to $95,000," the judge started to talk as soon as he came in the door.

"I knew it!" the lawyer exclaimed, "She was trying to set us up."

"Hold on there's more ... But, the defense will move to $125,000 if the plaintiff moves to $225,000."

"What does that do, puts $175,000 in the middle? Is that what she is looking for?" Gordon quizzed the mediator.

"You have to read the signals for yourself. You have the outside numbers right, and 175 is in the middle. Now, whether that is what Naomi is thinking, you take your own chances reading her mind. What do you think?" the mediator asked.

"I think it's a lot to have crammed down our throats. A middling value for this case would be $240,000, and we didn't even take a good look at that figure. We think that a dead minimum would be $190,000, and she isn't even close to that figure here," Getttem said.

"You do not have to respond to the conditional. If you don't like it, leave it alone. Respond to the base move to $95,000. Or you can edit the conditional, or even propose a new one yourself," said the mediator.

"OK, we would see her move to $125,000 and move to $275,000. Or we would move to $225,000 if she moves to $175,000. Otherwise, in response to her move to $95,000, we move to $301,000. How's that?" said the lawyer.

"Let's see what happens," said the judge as he started towards the other room.

Round 5 continued

The mediator repeated the offer Gordon Gettem had just given him as he entered the room and headed towards his seat. "Their formal move is to $301,000, but if you go to $125,000, they will go to $275,000. Or he would go to $225,000 if you move to $175,000."

"Interesting. He wants to center the thing at $200,000. Never going to happen." Naomi wrote some figures on her pad, and showed them to the taciturn insurance representative. "Has to be under that number," he said, pointing to some figures on Naomi's pad.

"Do you two need to talk? I can step out if you need," the mediator said.

"No, we've got it. We'll take the first conditional. We'll go to $125,000 if he goes to $275,000. So, we're there and it's his move." Naomi said.

"Uh, wouldn't it be back on your move?" the judge said.

"Maybe, but he changed our conditional, so that made it his move, and we accepted his move so it's back to him." Naomi said.

"I'm off."

Round 6

"They took your first conditional," the judge said as he came through the door "If you go to $275,000, they will go to $125,000. So, you are there, and it's your move."

"Alright. What do you suppose she has up her sleeve?"

"Only one way to find out."

"OK, let's try. We'll drop down to $250,000." Gettem said.

"Stand by, I doubt if this will take long." The mediator said as he headed to the door. He had not even unzipped his case.

Round 6 continued

The sandwiches had arrived, and Naomi and the claims manager were eating. "Help yourself, Martin," Naomi said, "they're taking a box in to Gordon right now."

The judge unwrapped the sandwich and got himself a fresh cup of coffee. "Gordon dropped down to $250,000," he said as he was moving about the room.

"OK, here is what I want to do. I am going to set up one of your famous descending sets of offers to get this thing nailed down at $175,000. As I get it, we are at $125,000 so this first move should be half the distance – which would be 25K, then next will be half that, or 13K, then half that or 6K or 7K, then half that or 3K. Right? Regardless of what Gordon moves." Naomi said.

"That's right. If I staged these right, you would move to $150,000 this time, then $163,000, then $170,000, then $173,000, then $174,500. Gordon will have the picture well before then." The judge said.

"OK let's do it. The move is to $150,000"

" Let's see what happens."

Rounds 7, 8 and 9

In Round 7, Gordon responded to Naomi's move to $150,000 by dropping down another $25,000 himself to $225,000. Naomi dropped the shoe by cutting the pattern move in approximately half to $13,000, and raising the defense offer $163,000.

In Round 8, Gordon knew something was afoot, but did not know where it was headed yet, so he pulled up sharply, dropping only $5,000 to $220,000, to see what was going on. Naomi made the third pattern move in the descending set by moving up $6,000 to $169,000.

The parties were at Round 9, and it was now Gordon's turn again. The mediator was waiting.

"I was hoping she was going to get to $200,000, but it looks like she is driving for $175,000." Gordon said.

"Can you see a pattern?" the mediator asked.

"Sure, it's your descending set. She is headed for $175,000, and at the rate she is going, she will never get there. Each move is half the value of the distance to the objective. She will never reach the objective." Gordon said.

"Well, that's the idea. Somewhere along the line the bidder makes an all-in call to end the set," the mediator said.

"I got it. Let me talk to my client for a minute."

The mediator stepped out, and the lawyer and his client talked quietly. Within a few minutes, Gettem motioned the mediator back into the room. "OK," he said, "we'll drop down $9,000 from $220,000 to $211,000. The demand is $211,000, down $9,000."

"Stand by," the mediator said, as he headed out the door

Round 9 continued

"What's he doing?" Naomi asked when she heard the judge explain the plaintiff's move.

"Is he resetting the midpoint?" the mediator asked.

"Aha, maybe, let's see." Naomi did a quick calculation. "I'll be; that's it," she said, "he was driving for a midpoint of $200,000, now he's aiming at $190,000. Well, I am not sure we have that much money, but let's play it out. Our move is up $3,000 to $172,000."

The judge was already on his way out the door.

Observe that the Delta or the difference between the two offers is now less than the cost of trial for both sides, and probably less than the cost of trial for just the defense side. Once figures get this close, it is a rare circumstance where the case does not settle.

Round 10

"And we will match that $3,000 and drop to $208,000" the plaintiff's lawyer said, as soon as the mediator got the message from the defense side out of his mouth.

He had not yet even sat down. The mediator turned on his heel and headed back to the defense room.

Round 10 continued

"Wow, that didn't take long. Were we right?" Naomi asked, as the judge came through the door.

"He came down $3,000. You are at $172,000, he is at $208,000. The middle is $190,000." The mediator sat down and unzipped his case.

"But we want him at $175,000. How do we get him there?" Naomi asked.

"This is always a war of nerves when it gets down to this point. You are $36,000 apart. Clearly, from an economic standpoint, you cannot afford to try this case over this difference, let alone the difference that is going to show up in a round or two. Can you? The question is, who is going to blink."

"Well, I don't think it's going to be us, I think I can tell you that. Bud, what do you think?" Naomi turned to the insurance rep. He made a sweep with his hand as though to brush away an annoying mosquito. "Run it out," he said.

Naomi looked at her notes, "Up $1,500 to $173,500. He cannot not get the message here," She said, intentionally stressing the double negative.

"I hear you, and will make sure that Gordon understands what you are saying," the mediator said as he headed to the door.

Round 11

The mediator repeated Naomi's move and sat back.

"OK, well how many moves do you think she will make here before throwing down the gauntlet and declaring herself? How far have you seen this go, Judge?" the lawyer asked.

"I would be surprised if she lets it go another round if she is going to declare. But then, I have been surprised before. Every one of these things are different," the mediator said.

"Have they had to call home office yet? Are they still within the authority that the claims guy brought with him?" the lawyer asked.

"I am not aware of any calls, but they have had plenty of opportunity when I'm not in there. And remember, Bud is a regional claims manager, not just an adjuster or claims specialist. He may well have the home office authority in his pocket," the judge said.

"Well, let's see what she is made of. Drop down $9,000 to $199,000. I'll break the $200,000 barrier and see what she really wants to do. Let's see if the $175,000 is a hard ending or just a penultimate target." The lawyer turned to his client, "We talked about this, right? You see where I am heading here, and you are OK with it?" The client nodded. Gordon turned back to the judge. OK, go," he said.

"Interesting move, Gordon. Should see something to clarify things." The judge headed for the hall.

Round 11 continued

"Well, here's the picture. You left it at $173,500 with Gordon at $208,000. Gordon sees your target at $175,000, believe me, I did not have to give him any cues or hints on this subject. With that in mind, here is his move. He is dropping down $9,000 to $199,000." The judge explained.

"Son of a … gun." Naomi said. "Well, we can call $175,000 last and final and let him take it or leave it."

"You can, but you have to mean it. If he calls you on it and heads for the elevators, you can't run after him with another offer – unless you want to cave all the way to $199,000."

"He can't call me on this. He can't litigate this thing for $25,000 any more than we can," Naomi said, "Can he?" She looked troubled.

"Maybe. You guys are looking at this cost avoidance issue from entirely different places; it's absolutely not the reverse of the same coin here. He's on a contingent fee and can afford to take some risk. Their costs are all in. The only thing they will go out of pocket for now will be the trial costs of the experts, and I understand he is going to use a video depo for one that is already in the can and paid for. You, on the other hand, are on the clock for every hour. You are going to burn through most of that $25,000 difference just in the next week or ten days in attorney fees alone, just getting this thing ready to go."

"You know the company line on this, the costs of litigation to the company plays no part in their evaluation of a case for settlement purposes," Naomi said, "They are obligated to their members."

The judge just looked at her. "Come on, Naomi, how long do you think I have been doing this?" he said.

"Oh, never mind. But do you think Gordon would walk?"

"Naomi, you have known Gordon as long as I have. I have seen him in court, and have worked ADR assignments with him, but I was never opposed to him when I was in private practice. He came into his own long after I took the bench, and I only know him from this side. You have to tell me – would he walk on this and try the case for the difference here?" the mediator said.

"Hmm, yeah, he just damn well might. Bud, what do you want to do – do you have another 25 grand in your pocket that you want to give Gordon to make him go away?" Naomi said.

"I have a little more," the insurance rep said. "I think he is looking at $190,000 but would probably take $185,000. Break through the $175,000 by a couple of thou and let's see what he does." This was the first complete sentence the mediator had heard come from the insurance representative's mouth all day.

"You're the boss. Judge, we'll go to $178,000. No message," Naomi said.

"I'm off to shake the box. This should be interesting." The mediator headed out the door.

Round 12

"Well, what do you think she said," the mediator asked as he came into the room and sat down.

"Did she say $175,000, last and final, take it or leave it?" Gordon said.

"Nope, that's what I expected. But she said, quote, $178,000, no message, close quote." The judge sat back.

"Hot damn! She blasted through her target. Let's not screw around here. Let's go to $198,000, down $1,000, but say if she offers $190,000 we'll accept." He turned to his client. "Is that alright?" Peter nodded his agreement. "Does this move make sense here?"

"It has to be your decision. Actually, the message you have been sending is that while Naomi was aiming at $175,000 you were aiming at $200,000 – and the actual midpoint between the two targets would be $187,500. But there are no rules here, so $190,000 is a very close call," The mediator said.

"Actually, I bet that Naomi tries for the $185,000, or Bud will want her to. And I have a move in mind that should end it." Gordon said. "Also, let's make sure we are not missing something. The deal will be all cash, new money, no offsets, to be paid to my trust account and to be available in a week. We will take care of all subrogated interests. Peter will provide a release and indemnity agreement, and Naomi and I will stipulate to a dismissal of the lawsuit with prejudice. I assume that is all that is required, and there are no other conditions or terms."

The judge had made notes as Gordon ran down the list of terms, and when Gordon finished, he stood up and headed for the door. "This shouldn't take long."

Round 12 continued

The judge sat down, unzipped his case and pulled out his notes. "In response to your move to $178,000, Gordon moved to $198,000 but said if you would offer $190,000, they would accept. He also wanted to cover that the settlement funds could be available in a week, and would be paid to his trust account. That Peter would provide a release and indemnity agreement. That Gordon's firm would see to it that all subrogated interests were satisfied. And that the lawsuit would be dismissed with prejudice.

"No, we don't have that much. Tell Gordon we have $185,000 and that's it. He has to take it or leave it, there isn't any more. All the other terms and conditions are OK. I think. Bud, can you get a check to me within a week?"

"Yeah, that's no problem," the insurance rep said, "and Judge, tell them that $185,000 is absolutely all that is available today. That's the reserves, it's what we had the case reserved at, and if we have to go any higher, I need home office approval. And in this case, anything above $185,000 requires approval by the home office claims committee and it triggers another level of reinsurance. We have to give notice to the reinsurers up the line. It's our call, but we have to notify the reinsurer that they're on the hook, and all this takes time. So, if he gives you any static about there being something extra at the home office if I just make the call, tell him I brought every nickel of the home office authority with me, and he's got it all at $185,000."

"I got it. All the other terms are as stated, no additional considerations?" the judge asked.

"Everything is as you said, nothing additional." Naomi turned to Bud. "We don't need a confidentiality agreement here?" Bud shook his head no.

"We're fine then," Naomi said.

The mediator finished his notes, zipped his case and headed out.

Round 13

"You called it," the judge said as he entered the room. The counter is a flat $185,000 with the message that this is all there is. The claims manager even spoke up and said it was the home office authority, that there wasn't any more without going back to committee, which would take time. All the other terms and conditions are fine, with nothing extra. So there it is: $185,000, best, last and final, your's to take it or leave."

Gordon had a big smile on his face. The case was not going to get away from him, and it was a good result. "What are your fees going to be Judge – for all of this. What's our half going to be?"

"Let's see, I have some hours at home, but let me figure this out." The mediator worked some figures out on his pad, and showed the paper to the lawyer. "This is a guess with what I have posted at home, but it's pretty close. Your share would be half that."

"That's what I figured. Tell Naomi and Bud we have a deal if they pay the entirety of the mediation fees. I know they are out of money in indemnity dollars, but the mediation fees come out of a different budget and he can add this little extra with no problem."

The move was no surprise to the judge. It had become almost a standard move for the very last touch to be to shift the entirety of the mediator's fee to the defense.

"I am going to write it up that way, and you sign it. Then I will take it down to Naomi, and if they agree, all they have to do is sign and it's done. If they don't like it, they can strike out the clause and I will bring it back for you to OK the strike out. How's that?" the mediator suggested.

"Good. Go ahead."

The mediator wrote out a paragraph explaining the deal on a yellow pad. "Here, do you think it needs anything else?" He handed the pad to Gordon.

"Nope," Gordon said, reading, "that's it."

"Go ahead and sign it, and have your client sign, and I will take it back for the defense reaction." Both Gordon and his client signed the handwritten page and handed it to the judge.

"Back in a minute," he said as he headed for the door.

Round 12 continued

"One tweak," the judge said as he entered the room holding up the yellow pad with the signed page on top. "The standard plaintiff's response to the last move by a defendant: The deal is accepted if you pay the entirety of the mediation fee."

He tossed the yellow pad onto the table. "You are close enough here that I wrote it up and had them sign it. If you agree, just sign that thing and we can go home. If you don't agree with the tweak, strike it out, initial the strike out and sign the agreement, and I'll take it back and see if they will approve the deal without."

"What are your fees, Martin?" Naomi asked.

"Here's what I showed Gordon." The mediator showed Naomi the figures he put together. "This is pretty close if you get this done within the present hour. If you need to haggle some more over this, it could be more."

"Bud?" Naomi turned to the claims manager.

"That's fine, Naomi, let's get it done. You invoice the fee to me as a cost and I can pay it entirely out of the cost budget. It's not for indemnity so it doesn't need to go to committee and I don't need Carl's approval. So, go ahead and sign her up as is. Good job, Judge, Thank you very much."

"We've both signed," Naomi said, "I'll take this over and get copies made."

"Good. I will go tell Gordon that it's a done deal. Thanks, everybody."

Rd	Plaintiff	Defense	Midpoint	Difference
1	447,525	$45,000	$246,263	$403,525
2	397,525	70,000	233,763	327,525
3	350,000	94,000	222,000	253,000
4	302,000	95,000/* [125/225]	183,500	204,000
5	301,000/*[275/125]	*Accepts Bracket	200,000	150,000
	*275,000	*125,000		
6	250,000	150,000	200,000	100,000
7	225,000	163,000	194,000	62,000
8	220,000	169,000	194,500	51,000
9	211,000	172,000	191,500	39,000
10	208,000	173,500	190,750	34,500
11	199,000	178,000	188,500	21,000
12	198/*190,000	185,000 LBF	---	5,000
13	Accepts/Mediator fee	Accepts		

About the Author

Judge Duff McKee is a retired district court trial judge on senior status, engaged in providing alternative dispute resolution services throughout Idaho and adjoining states. He was honored by Idaho State Bar with its Professionalism award in 2011. He is a graduate of the University of Idaho College of Law and has been a member of the Idaho Bar for over 52 years. He lives and practices in Boise, and claims to be a fifth generation native of Idaho – his great-great grandfather pioneered to what became the Idaho Territory in the 1860s. He is married, and dotes on five grandchildren.

Made in the USA
Monee, IL
04 November 2026

67381855R00128